ISBN 0-8373-2044-5

C-2044   CAREER EXAMINATION SERIES

This is your
PASSBOOK® for...

Maintenance Supervisor

Test Preparation Study Guide

Questions & Answers

NLC
NATIONAL LEARNING CORPORATION

Copyright © 2004 by

National Learning Corporation

212 Michael Drive, Syosset, New York 11791

(516) 921-8888
Outside N.Y.: 1(800) 645-6337
ORDER FAX: 1(516) 921-8743
www.passbooks.com
email: passbooks @ aol.com
sales @ passbooks.com
info @ passbooks.com

PRINTED IN THE UNITED STATES OF AMERICA

PASSBOOK®
NOTICE

This book is *SOLELY* intended for, is sold *ONLY* to, and its use is *RESTRICTED* to *individual*, bona fide applicants or candidates who qualify by virtue of having seriously filed applications for appropriate license, certificate, professional and/or promotional advancement, higher school matriculation, scholarship, or other legitimate requirements of educational and/or governmental authorities.

This book is *NOT* intended for use, class instruction, tutoring, training, duplication, copying, reprinting, excerption, or adaptation, etc., by:

    (1) Other Publishers
    (2) Proprietors and/or Instructors of "Coaching" and/or Preparatory Courses
    (3) Personnel and/or Training Divisions of commercial, industrial, and governmental organizations
    (4) Schools, colleges, or universities and/or their departments and staffs, including teachers and other personnel
    (5) Testing Agencies or Bureaus
    (6) Study groups which seek by the purchase of a single volume to copy and/or duplicate and/or adapt this material for use by the group as a whole without having purchased individual volumes for each of the members of the group
    (7) Et al.

Such persons would be in violation of appropriate Federal and State statutes.

PROVISION OF LICENSING AGREEMENTS. — Recognized educational commercial, industrial, and governmental institutions and organizations, and others legitimately engaged in educational pursuits, including training, testing, and measurement activities, may address a request for a licensing agreement to the copyright owners, who will determine whether, and under what conditions, including fees and charges, the materials in this book may be used by them. In other words, a licensing facility *exists* for the legitimate use of the material in this book on other than an individual basis. However, it is asseverated and affirmed here that the materials in this book *CANNOT* be used without the receipt of the express permission of such a licensing agreement from the Publishers.

NATIONAL LEARNING CORPORATION
212 Michael Drive
Syosset, New York 11791

Inquiries re licensing agreements should be addressed to:
    The President
    National Learning Corporation
    212 Michael Drive
    Syosset, New York 11791

PASSBOOK SERIES®

THE *PASSBOOK SERIES®* has been created to prepare applicants and candidates for the ultimate academic battlefield—the examination room.

At some time in our lives, each and every one of us may be required to take an examination—for validation, matriculation, admission, qualification, registration, certification, or licensure.

Based on the assumption that every applicant or candidate has met the basic formal educational standards, has taken the required number of courses, and read the necessary texts, the *PASSBOOK SERIES®* furnishes the one special preparation which may assure passing with confidence, instead of failing with insecurity. Examination questions— together with answers—are furnished as the basic vehicle for study so that the mysteries of the examination and its compounding difficulties may be eliminated or diminished by a sure method.

This book is meant to help you pass your examination provided that you qualify and are serious in your objective.

The entire field is reviewed through the huge store of content information which is succinctly presented through a provocative and challenging approach—the question-and-answer method.

A climate of success is established by furnishing the correct answers at the end of each test.

You soon learn to recognize types of questions, forms of questions, and patterns of questioning. You may even begin to anticipate expected outcomes.

You perceive that many questions are repeated or adapted so that you gain acute insights, which may enable you to score many sure points.

You learn how to confront new questions, or types of questions, and to attack them confidently and work out the correct answers.

You note objectives and emphases, and recognize pitfalls and dangers, so that you may make positive educational adjustments.

Moreover, you are kept fully informed in relation to new concepts, methods, practices, and directions in the field.

You discover that you are actually taking the examination all the time: you are preparing for the examination by "taking" an examination, not by reading extraneous and/or supererogatory textbooks.

In short, this PASSBOOK®, used directedly, should be an important factor in helping you to pass your test.

MAINTENANCE SUPERVISOR

DUTIES

Supervise the building maintenance of small State institutions. On smaller construction, repair, and alteration projects, Maintenance Supervisors prepare plans and specifications, costs estimates, and lists of material required. On larger projects, they prepare drafts, sketches, or estimates to be used in construction with preparation of detailed plans. They supervise all work in the execution of plans, estimate materials and labor; and lay out work and assign subordinates to various tasks. They instruct subordinates in general building construction and maintenance and regularly inspect work progress. They prepare reports and conduct studies of mechanical and maintenance needs; and coordinate mechanical services and construction projects with other institutional programs.

SCOPE OF THE EXAMINATION

The written test is designed to test for knowledge, skills and/or abilities in such areas as:

1. BUILDING MAINTENANCE AND REPAIR;
2. BUILDING TRADES, INCLUDING MECHANICAL AND ELECTRICAL;
3. GROUNDS MAINTENANCE;
4. OPERATION AND MAINTENANCE OF HEATING, VENTILATION AND AIR CONDITIONING SYSTEMS—These questions test for knowledge of basic principles, practices and techniques essential to the correct operation and maintenance of heating, ventilating and air conditioning systems;
5. REVIEW AND INTERPRETATION OF PLANS AND SPECIFICATIONS, THE PREPARATION OF ESTIMATES, AND OVERSIGHT OF CONTRACT COMPLIANCE;
6. WORK SCHEDULING; and
7. SUPERVISION—These questions test for knowledge of the principles and practices employed in planning, organizing and controlling the activities of a work unit toward predetermined objectives. The concepts covered, usually in a situational question format, include such topics as assigning and reviewing work; evaluating performance; maintaining work standards; motivating and developing subordinates; implementing procedural change; increasing efficiency; and dealing with problems of absenteeism, morale and discipline.

HOW TO TAKE A TEST

I. YOU MUST PASS AN EXAMINATION

A. *WHAT EVERY CANDIDATE SHOULD KNOW*

Examination applicants often ask us for help in preparing for the written test. What can I study in advance? What kinds of questions will be asked? How will the test be given? How will the papers be graded?

As an applicant for a civil service examination, you may be wondering about some of these things. Our purpose here is to suggest effective methods of advance study and to describe civil service examinations.

Your chances for success on this examination can be increased if you know how to prepare. Those "pre-examination jitters" can be reduced if you know what to expect. You can even experience an adventure in good citizenship if you know why civil service examinations are given.

B. *WHY ARE CIVIL SERVICE EXAMINATIONS GIVEN?*

Civil service examinations are important to you in two ways. As a citizen, you want public jobs filled by employees who know how to do their work. As a job-seeker, you want a fair chance to compete for that job on an equal footing with other candidates. The best known means of accomplishing this two-fold goal is the competitive examination.

Examinations are widely publicized throughout the nation. They may be administered for jobs in federal, state, city, municipal, town, or village governments or agencies.

Any citizen may apply, with some limitations, such as the age or residence of applicants. Your experience and education may be reviewed to see whether you meet the requirements for the particular examination. When these requirements exist, they are reasonable and are applied consistently to all applicants. Thus, a competitive examination may cause you some uneasiness now, but it is your privilege and safeguard.

C. *HOW ARE CIVIL SERVICE EXAMINATIONS DEVELOPED?*

Examinations are carefully written by trained technicians who are specialists in the field known as "psychological measurement," in consultation with recognized authorities in the field of work that the test will cover. These experts recommend the subject matter areas or skills to be tested; only those knowledges or skills important to your success on the job are included. The most reliable books and source materials available are used as references. Together, the experts and technicians judge the difficulty level of the questions.

Test technicians know how to phrase questions so that the problem is clearly stated. Their ethics do not permit "trick" or "catch" questions. Questions may have been tried out on sample groups, or subjected to statistical analysis, to determine their usefulness.

Written tests are often used in combination with performance tests, ratings of training and experience, and oral interviews. All of these measures combine to form the best known means of finding the right man for the right job.

II. HOW TO PASS THE WRITTEN TEST

A. *NATURE OF THE EXAMINATION*

To prepare intelligently for civil service examinations, you should know how they differ from school examinations you have taken. In school you were assigned certain definite pages to read or subjects to cover. The examination questions were quite detailed and usually emphasized memory. Civil service examinations, on the other hand, try to discover your present ability to perform the duties of a position, plus your potentiality to learn these duties. In other words, a civil service examination attempts to predict how successful you will be. Questions cover such a broad area that they cannot be as minute and detailed as school examination questions.

In the public service similar kinds of work, or positions, are grouped together in one "class." This process is known as "position-classification." All the positions in a class are paid according to the salary range for that class. One class title covers all these positions, and they are all tested by the same examination.

B. *FOUR BASIC STEPS*

1. Study the Announcement.--How, then, can you know what subjects to study? Our best answer is: "Learn as much as possible about the class of positions for which you have applied." The examination will test the knowledge, skills, and abilities needed to do the work.

Your most valuable source of information about the position you want is the official announcement of the examination. This announcement lists the training and experience qualifications. Check these standards and apply only if you come reasonably close to meeting them.

The brief description of the position in the examination announcement offers some clues to the subjects which will be tested. Think about the job itself. Review the duties in your mind. Can you perform them, or are there some in which you are rusty? Fill in the blank spots in your preparation.

Many jurisdictions preview the written test in the examination announcement by including a section called "Knowledge and Abilities Required," "Scope of Examination," or some similar heading. Here you will find out specifically what fields will be tested.

2. Review Your Own Background.-- Once you learn in general what the position is all about, and what you need to know to do the work, ask yourself which subjects you already know fairly well and which need improvement. You may wonder whether to concentrate on improving your strong areas or on building some background in your fields of weakness. When the announcement has specified "some knowledge" or "considerable knowledge," or has used adjectives such as "beginning principles of ...." or "advanced .....methods," you can get a clue as to the number and difficulty of questions to be asked in any given field. More questions, and hence broader coverage, would be included for those subjects which are more important in the work. Now weigh your strengths and weaknesses against the job requirements and prepare accordingly.

3. Determine the Level of the Position.-- Another way to tell how intensively you should prepare is to understand the level of the job for which you are applying. Is it the entering level? In other words, is this the position in which beginners in a field of work are hired? Or is it an intermediate or advanced level? Sometimes this is indicated by such words as "Junior" or "Senior" in the class title.Other jurisdictions use Roman numerals to designate the level: Clerk I,

Clerk II, for example. The word "Supervisor" sometimes appears in the title. If the level is not indicated by the title, check the description of duties. Will you be working under very close supervision, or will you have responsibility for independent decisions in this work?

4. Choose Appropriate Study Materials.-- Now that you know the subjects to be examined and the relative amount of each subject to be covered, you can choose suitable study materials. For beginning level jobs, or even advanced ones, if you have a pronounced weakness in some aspect of your training, read a modern, standard textbook in that field. Be sure it is up-to-date and has general coverage. Such books are normally available at your library, and the librarian will be glad to help you locate one. For entry level positions, questions of appropriate difficulty are chosen -- neither highly advanced questions, nor those too simple. Such questions require careful thought but not advanced training.

If the position for which you are applying is technical or advanced, you will read more advanced, specialized material. If you are already familiar with the basic principles of your field, elementary textbooks would waste your time. Concentrate on advanced textbooks and technical periodicals. Think through the concepts and review difficult problems in your field.

These are all general sources. You can get more ideas on your own initiative, following these leads. For example, training manuals and publications of the government agency which employs workers in your field can be useful, particularly for technical and professional positions. A letter or visit to the government department involved may result in more specific study suggestions, and certainly will provide you with a more definite idea of the exact nature of the position you are seeking.

II. KINDS OF TESTS

Tests are used for purposes other than measuring knowledge and ability to perform specified duties. For some positions, it is equally important to test ability to make adjustments to new situations or to profit from training. In others, basic mental abilities not dependent upon information are essential. Questions which test these things may not appear as pertinent to the duties of the position as those which test for knowledge and information. Yet they are often highly important parts of a fair examination. For very general questions, it is almost impossible to help you direct your study efforts. What we can do is to point out some of the more common of these general abilities needed in public service positions and describe some typical questions.

1. General Information

Broad, general information has been found useful for predicting job success in some kinds of work. This is tested in a variety of ways, from vocabulary lists to questions about current events. Basic background in some field of work, such as sociology or economics, may be sampled in a group of questions. Often these are principles which have become familiar to most persons through "exposure" rather than through formal training. It is difficult to advise you how to study for these questions; being alert to the world around you is our best suggestion.

3

2. Verbal Ability

An example of an ability needed in many positions is verbal or language ability. Verbal ability is, in brief, the ability to use and understand words. Vocabulary and grammar tests are typical measures of this ability. "Reading comprehension" or "paragraph interpretation" questions are common in many kinds of civil service tests. You are given a paragraph of written material and asked to find its central meaning.

3. Numerical Ability

Number skills can be tested by the familiar arithmetic problem, by checking paired lists of numbers to see which are alike and which are different, or by interpreting charts and graphs. In the latter test, a graph may be printed in the test booklet which you are asked to use as the basis for answering questions.

4. Observation

A popular test for law-enforcement positions is the observation test. A picture is shown to you for several minutes, then taken away. Questions about the picture test your ability to observe both details and larger elements.

5. Following Directions

In many positions in the public service, the employee must be able to carry out written instructions dependably and accurately. You may be given a chart with several columns, each column listing a variety of information. The questions require you to carry out directions involving the information given in the chart.

6. Skills and Aptitudes

Performance tests effectively measure some manual skills and aptitudes. When the skill is one in which you are trained, such as typing or shorthand, you can practice. These tests are often very much like those given in business school or high school courses. For many of the other skills and aptitudes, however, no short-time preparation can be made. Skills and abilities natural to you or that you have developed throughout your lifetime are being tested.

Many of the general questions just described provide all the data needed to answer the questions and ask you to use your reasoning ability to find the answers. Your best preparation for these tests, as well as for tests of facts and ideas, is to be at your physical and mental best. You, no doubt, have your own methods of getting into an exam-taking mood and keeping "in shape." The next section lists some ideas on this subject.

IV. KINDS OF QUESTIONS

Only rarely is the "essay" question, which you answer in narrative form, used in civil service tests. Civil service tests are usually of the short-answer type. Full instructions for answering these questions will be given to you at the examination. But in case this is your first experience with short-answer questions and separate answer sheets, here is what you need to know.

1. Multiple-Choice Questions

Most popular of the short-answer questions is the "multiple-choice" or "best-answer" question. It can be used, for example, to test for factual knowledge, ability to solve problems, or judgment in meeting situations found at work.

A multiple-choice question is normally one of three types:

(1) It can begin with an incomplete statement followed by several possible endings. You are to find the one ending which *best* completes the statement, although some of the others may not be entirely wrong.

(2) It can also be a complete statement in the form of a question which is answered by choosing one of the statements listed.

(3) It can be in the form of a problem -- again you select the best answer.

Here is an example of a multiple-choice question with a discussion which should give you some clues as to the method for choosing the right answer.

SAMPLE QUESTION:

When an employee has a complaint about his assignment, the action which will *best* help him overcome his difficulty is

    (A) to discuss his difficulty with his co-workers
    (B) to take the problem to the head of the organization
    (C) to take the problem to the person who gave him the assignment
    (D) to say nothing to anyone about his complaint

In answering this question you should study each of the choices to find which is best. Consider choice (A). Certainly an employee may discuss his complaint with fellow employees, but no change or improvement can result, and the complaint remains unsolved. Choice (B) is a poor choice since the head of the organization probably does not know what assignment you have been given, and taking your problem to him is known as "going over the head" of the supervisor. The supervisor, or person who made the assignment, is the person who can clarify it or correct any injustice. Choice (C) is, therefore, correct. To say nothing, as in choice (D), is unwise. Supervisors have an interest in knowing the problems employees are facing, and the employee is seeking a solution to his problem.

  2. True-False Questions

The "true-false" or "right-wrong" form of question is sometimes used. Here a complete statement is given. Your problem is to decide whether the statement is right or wrong.

SAMPLE QUESTION:

A person-to-person long distance telephone call costs less than a station-to-station call to the same city.

This question is wrong, or "false," since person-to-person calls are more expensive.

This is not a complete list of all possible question forms, although most of the others are variations of these common types. You will always get complete directions for answering questions. Be sure you understand *how* to mark your answers -- ask questions until you do.

V. RECORDING YOUR ANSWERS

For an examination with very few applicants, you may be told to record your answers in the test booklet itself. Separate answer sheets are much more common. If this separate answer sheet is to be scored by machine -- and this is often the case -- it is highly important that you mark your answers correctly in order to get credit.

An electric test-scoring machine is often used in civil service offices because of the speed with which papers can be scored. Machine-scored answer sheets must be marked with a special pencil, which will be given to you. This pencil has a high graphite content which responds to the electrical scoring machine. As a matter of fact, stray dots may register as answers, so do not let your pencil rest on the answer sheet while you are pondering the correct answer. Also, if your pencil lead breaks or is otherwise defective, ask for another.

Since the answer sheet will be dropped in a slot in the scoring machine, be careful not to bend the corners or get the paper crumpled.

The answer sheet normally has five vertical columns of numbers, with 30 numbers to a column. These numbers correspond to the question numbers in your test booklet. After each number, going across the page, are four or five pairs of dotted lines. These short dotted lines have small letters or numbers above them. The first two pairs may also have a "T" and "F" above the letters. This indicates that the first two pairs only are to be used if the questions are of the true-false type. If the questions are multiple-choice, disregard this "T" and "F" completely, and pay attention only to the small number or letters.

Answer your questions in the manner of the sample that follows. Proceed in the sequential steps outlined below.

Assume that you are answering question 32, which is:

32. The largest city in the United States is:
    A. Washington, D.C.   B. New York City   C. Chicago
    D. Detroit   E. San Francisco

1. Choose the answer you think is best.
    New York City is the largest, so choice B is correct.
2. Find the row of dotted lines numbered the same as the question you are answering.
    This is question number 32, so find row number 32.
3. Find the pair of dotted lines corresponding to the answer you have chosen.
    You have chosen answer B, so find the pair of dotted lines marked "B".
4. Make a solid black mark between the dotted lines.
    Go up and down two or three times with your pencil so plenty of graphite rubs off, but do not let the mark get outside or above the dots.

VI. BEFORE THE TEST

Common sense will help you find procedures to follow to get ready for an examination. Too many of us, however, overlook these sensible measures. Indeed, nervousness and fatigue have been found to be the most serious reasons why applicants fail to do their best on civil service tests. Here is a list of reminders.

1. Begin Your Preparation Early

Don't wait until the last minute to go scurrying around for books and materials or to find out what the position is all about.

2. Prepare Continuously

An hour a night for a week is better than an all-night cram session. This has been definitely established. What is more, a night a week for a month will return better dividends than crowding your study into a shorter period of time.

3. Locate the Place of the Examination

You have been sent a notice telling you when and where to report for the examination. If the location is in a different town or otherwise unfamiliar to you, it would be well to inquire the best route and learn something about the building.

4. Relax the Night Before the Test

Allow your mind to rest. Do not study at all that night. Plan some mild recreation or diversion; then go to bed early and get a good night's sleep.

5. Get Up Early Enough to Make a Leisurely Trip to the Place for the Test

Then unforeseen events, traffic snarls, unfamiliar buildings, will not upset you.

6. Dress Comfortably

A written test is not a fashion show. You will be known by number and not by name, so wear something comfortable.

7. Leave Excess Paraphernalia at Home

Shopping bags and odd bundles will get in your way. You need bring only the items mentioned in the official notice sent to you; usually everything you need is provided. Do not bring reference books to the examination. They will only confuse those last minutes and be taken away from you when in the test room.

8. Arrive Somewhat Ahead of Time

If because of transportation schedules you must get there very early, bring a newspaper or magazine to take your mind off yourself while waiting.

9. Locate the Examination Room

When you have found the proper room, you will be directed to the seat or part of the room where you will sit. Sometimes you are given a sheet of instructions to read while you are waiting. Do not fill out any forms until you are told to do so; just read them and be ready.

10. Relax and Prepare to Listen to the Instructions

11. If you have any physical problem that may keep you from doing your best, be sure to tell the test administrator. If you are sick, or in poor health, you really cannot do your best on the test. You can come back and take the test some other time.

VII. AT THE TEST

The day of the test is here and you have the test booklet in your hand. The temptation to get going is very strong. Caution! There is more to success than knowing the right answers. You must know how to identify your papers and understand variations in the type of short-answer question used in this particular examination. Follow these suggestions for maximum results from your efforts:

1. Cooperate with the Monitor

The test administrator has a duty to create a situation in which you can be as much at ease as possible. He will give instructions, tell you when to begin, check to see that you are marking your answer sheet correctly. He is not there to guard you, although he will see that your competitors do not take unfair advantage. He wants to help you do your best.

2. Listen to All Instructions

Don't jump the gun! Wait until you understand all directions. In most civil service tests you get more time than you need to answer the questions. So don't get in a hurry. Read each word of instructions until you clearly understand the meaning. Study the examples. Listen to all announcements. Follow directions. Ask questions if you do not understand what to do.

3. Identify Your Papers

Civil service examinations are usually identified by number only. You will be assigned a number; you must not put your name on your test papers. Be sure to copy your number correctly. Since more than one examination may be given, copy your exact examination title.

4. Plan Your Time

Unless you are told that a test is a "speed" or "rate-of-work" test, speed itself is not usually important. Time enough to answer all the questions will be provided. But this does not mean that you have all day. An overall time limit has been set. Divide the total time (in minutes) by the number of questions to get the approximate time you have for each question.

5. Do Not Linger Over Difficult Questions

If you come across a difficult question, mark it with a paper clip (useful to have along) and come back to it when you have been through the booklet. One caution if you do this -- be sure to skip a number on your answer sheet too. Check often to be sure that you have not lost your place and that you are marking in the row numbered the same as the question you are answering.

6. Read the Questions

Be sure you know what the question asks! Many capable people are unsuccessful because they failed to *read* the questions correctly.

7. Answer All Questions

Unless you have been instructed that a penalty will be deducted for incorrect answers, it is better to guess than to omit a question.

8. Speed Tests

It is often better *not* to guess on speed tests. It has been found that on timed tests people are tempted to spend the last few seconds before time is called in marking answers at random -- without even reading them -- in the hope of picking up a few extra points. To discourage this practice, the instructions may warn you that your score will be "corrected" for guessing. That is, a penalty will be applied. The incorrect answers will be deducted from the correct ones, or some other penalty formula will be used.

9. Review Your Answers

If you finish before time is called, go back to the questions you guessed or omitted to give further thought to them. Review other answers if you have time.

10. Return Your Test Materials

If you are ready to leave before others have finished or time is called, take *all* your materials to the monitor and leave quietly. Never take any test material with you. The monitor can discover whose papers are not complete, and taking a test booklet may be grounds for disqualification.

III. EXAMINATION TECHNIQUES

1. Read the *general* instructions carefully. These are usually printed on the first page of the examination booklet. As a rule, these instructions refer to the timing of the examination; the fact that you should not start work until the signal and must stop work at a signal, etc. If there are any *special* instructions, such as a choice of questions to be answered, make sure that you note this instruction carefully.

2. When you are ready to start work on the examination, that is as soon as the signal has been given, read the instructions to each question booklet, underline any key words or phrases, such as *least, best, outline, describe,* and the like. In this way you will tend to answer as requested rather than discover on reviewing your paper that you *listed without describing,* that you selected the *worst* choice rather than the *best* choice, etc.

3. If the examination is of the objective or so-called multiple-choice type, that is, each question will also give a series of possible answers: A, B, C, or D, and you are called upon to select the best answer and write the letter next to that answer on your answer paper, it is advisable to start answering each question in turn. There may be anywhere from 50 to 100 such questions in the three or four hours allotted and you can see how much time would be taken if you read through all the questions before beginning to answer any. Furthermore, if you come across a question or a group of questions which you know would be difficult to answer, it would undoubtedly affect your handling of all the other questions.

4. If the examination is of the esssay-type and contains but a few questions, it is a moot point as to whether you should read all the questions before starting to answer any one. Of course if you are given a choice, say five out of seven and the like, then it is essential to read all the questions so you can eliminate the two which are most difficult. If, however, you are asked to answer all the questions, there may be danger in trying to answer the easiest one first because you may find that you will spend too much time on it. The best technique is to answer the first question, then proceed to the second, etc.

5. Time your answers. Before the examination begins, write down the time it started, then add the time allowed for the examination and write down the time it must be completed, then divide the time available somewhat as follows:

(a) If 3½ hours are allowed, that would be 210 minutes. If you have 80 objective-type questions, that would be an average of 2½ minutes per question. Allow yourself no more than 2 minutes per question, or a total of 160 minutes, which will permit about 50 minutes to review.

(b) If for the time allotment of 210 minutes, there are 7 essay questions to answer, that would average about 30 minutes a question. Give yourself only 25 minutes per question so that you have about 35 minutes to review.

6. The most important instruction is *to read each question* and make sure you know what is wanted. The second most important instruction is to *time yourself properly* so that you answer every question. The third most important instruction is to *answer every question.* Guess if you have to but include something for each question. Remember that you will receive no credit for a blank and will probably receive some credit if you write something in answer to an essay question. If you guess a letter, say "B" for a multiple-choice question, you may have guessed right. If you leave a blank as the answer to a multiple-choice question, the examiners may respect your feelings but it will not add a point to your score.

7. Suggestions
   a. <u>Objective-Type Questions</u>
      (1) Examine the question booklet for proper sequence of pages and questions.
      (2) Read all instructions carefully.
      (3) Skip any question which seems too difficult; return to it after all other questions have been answered.
      (4) Apportion your time properly; do not spend too much time on any single question or group of questions.
      (5) Note and underline key words -- *all, most, fewest, least, best, worst, same, opposite.*
      (6) Pay particular attention to negatives.
      (7) Note unusual option, e.g., unduly long, short, complex, different or similar in content to the body of the question.
      (8) Observe the use of "hedging" words -- *probably, may, most likely, etc.*
      (9) Make sure that your answer is put next to the same number as the question.
      (10) Do not second-guess unless you have good reason to believe the second answer is definitely more correct.
      (11) Cross out original answer if you decide another answer is more accurate; do not erase.
      (12) Answer all questions; guess unless instructed otherwise.
      (13) Leave time for review.
   b. <u>Essay-Type Questions</u>
      (1) Read each question carefully.
      (2) Determine exactly what is wanted. Underline key words or phrases.
      (3) Decide on outline or paragraph answer.
      (4) Include many different points and elements unless asked to develop any one or two points or elements.
      (5) Show impartiality by giving pros and cons unless directed to select one side only.
      (6) Make and write down any assumptions you find necessary to answer the question.
      (7) Watch your English, grammar, punctuation, choice of words.
      (8) Time your answers; don't crowd material.

8. Answering the Essay Question
   Most essay questions can be answered by framing the specific response around several key words or ideas. Here are a few such key words or ideas:

M's: manpower, materials, methods, money, management;
P's: purpose, program, policy, plan, procedure, practice, problems, pitfalls, personnel, public relations.

a. Six Basic Steps in Handling Problems:
  (1) Preliminary plan and background development
  (2) Collect information, data and facts
  (3) Analyze and interpret information, data and facts
  (4) Analyze and develop solutions as well as make recommendations
  (5) Prepare report and sell recommendations
  (6) Install recommendations and follow up effectiveness

b. Pitfalls to Avoid
  (1) *Taking things for granted*
      A statement of the situation does not necessarily imply that each of the elements is necessarily true; for example, a complaint may be invalid and biased so that all that can be taken for granted is that a complaint has been registered.
  (2) *Considering only one side of a situation*
      Wherever possible, indicate several alternatives and then point out the reasons you selected the best one.
  (3) *Failing to indicate follow-up*
      Whenever your answer indicates action on your part, make certain that you will take proper follow-up action to see how successful your recommendations, procedures, or actions turn out to be.
  (4) *Taking too long in answering any single question*
      Remember to time your answers properly.

IX. AFTER THE TEST
  Scoring procedures differ in detail among civil service jurisdictions although the general principles are the same. Whether the papers are hand-scored or graded by the electric scoring machine we have described, they are nearly always graded by number. That is, the person who marks the paper knows only the number -- never the name -- of the applicant. Not until all the papers have been graded will they be matched with names. If other tests, such as training and experience or oral interview ratings have been given, scores will be combined. Different parts of the examination usually have different weights. For example, the written test might count 60 percent of the final grade, and a rating of training and experience 40 percent. In many jurisdictions, veterans will have a certain number of points added to their grades.
  After the final grade has been determined, the names are placed in grade order and an eligible list is established. There are various methods for resolving ties between those who get the same final grade: probably the most common is to place first the name of the person whose application was received first. Job offers are made from the eligible list in the order the names appear on it.
  You will be notified of your grade and your rank order as soon as all these computations have been made. This will be done as rapidly as possible.
  People who are found to meet the requirements in the announcement are called "eligibles." Their names are put on a list of eligibles. An eligible's chances of getting a job depend on how high he stands on this list and how fast agencies are filling jobs from the list.

When a job is to be filled from a list of eligibles, the agency asks for the names of people on the list of eligibles for that job.

When the civil service commission receives this request, it sends to the agency the names of the three people highest on the list. Or, if the job to be filled has specialized requirements, the office sends the agency, from the general list, the names of the top three persons who meet those requirements.

The appointing officer makes a **choice from among** the three people whose names were sent to him. If **the selected** person accepts the appointment, the names of the others **are** put back on the list to be considered for future openings.

That is the rule in hiring from all kinds of eligible lists, whether they are for typist, carpenter, chemist, or something else. For every vacancy, the appointing officer has his choice of any one of the top three eligibles on the list. This explains why the person whose name is on top of the list sometimes does not get an appointment when some of the persons lower on the list do. If the appointing officer chooses the No.2 or No.3 eligible, the No.1 eligible does not get a job at once, but stays on the list until he is appointed or the list is terminated.

X. HOW TO PASS THE INTERVIEW TEST

The examination for which you applied requires an oral interview test. You have already taken the written test and you are now being called for the interview test -- the final part of the formal examination.

You may think that it is not possible to prepare for an interview test and that there are no procedures to follow during an interview.

Our purpose is to point out some things you can do in advance that will help you and some good rules to follow and pitfalls to avoid while you are being interviewed.

A. WHAT IS AN INTERVIEW SUPPOSED TO TEST?

The written examination is designed to test the technical knowledge and competence of the candidate; the oral is designed to evaluate intangible qualities, not readily measured otherwise, and to establish a list showing the relative fitness of each candidate, *as measured against his competitors,* for the position sought. Scoring is not on the basis of "right" or "wrong," but on a sliding scale of values ranging from "not passable" to "outstanding." As a matter of fact, it is possible to achieve a relatively low score without a single "incorrect" answer because of evident weakness in the qualities being measured,

Occasionally, an examination may consist entirely of an oral test -- either an individual or a group oral. In such cases, information is sought concerning the technical knowledges and abilities of the candidate, since there has been no written examination for this purpose. More commonly, however, an oral test is used to supplement a written examination.

B. WHO CONDUCTS INTERVIEWS?

The composition of oral boards varies among different jurisdictions. **In nearly all,** a representative of the personnel department **serves as chairman.** One of the members of the board may be a representative **of the d**epartment in which the candidate would work. In **some cases,** "outside experts" are used, and, frequently, a business **man or some** other representative of the general public is asked to serve. Labor and management or other special groups may be represented. The aim is to secure the services of experts in the appropriate field.

However the board is composed, it is a good idea (and not at all improper or unethical) to ascertain in advance of the interview who the members are and what groups they represent. When you are introduced to them, you will have some idea of their backgrounds and interests, and at least you will not stutter and stammer over their names.

C. *WHAT TO DO BEFORE THE INTERVIEW*

While knowledge about the board members is useful and takes some of the surprise element out of the interview, there is other preparation which is more substantive. It *is* possible to prepare for an oral -- in several ways:

1. Keep a Copy of Your Application and Review it Carefully Before the Interview

   This may be the only document before the oral board, and the starting point of the interview. Know what experience and education you have listed there, and the sequence and dates of it. Sometimes the board will ask *you* to review the highlights of your experience for them; you should not have to hem and haw doing it.

2. Study the Class Specification and the Examination Announcement

   Usually, the oral board has one or both of these to guide them. The qualities, characteristics, or knowledges required by the position sought are stated in these documents. They offer valuable clues as to the nature of the oral interview. For example, if the job involves supervisory responsibilities, the announcement will usually indicate that knowledge of modern supervisory methods and the qualifications of the candidate as a supervisor will be tested. If so, you can expect such questions, frequently in the form of a hypothetical situation which you are expected to solve. *Never* go into an oral without knowledge of the duties and responsibilities of the job you seek.

3. Think Through Each Qualification Required

   Try to visualize the kind of questions *you* would ask if you were a board member. How well could you answer them? Try especially to appraise your own knowledge and background in each area, *measured against the job sought*, and identify any areas in which you are weak. Be critical and realistic -- do not flatter yourself.

4. Do Some General Reading in Areas in Which You Feel You May be Weak

   For example, if the job involves supervision and your past experience has *not*, some general reading in supervisory methods and practices, particularly in the field of human relations, might be useful. *Do not* study agency procedures or detailed manuals. The oral board will be testing your understanding and capacity, *not* your memory.

5. Get a Good Night's Sleep and Watch Your General Health and Mental Attitude

   You will want a clear head at the interview. Take care of a cold or other minor ailment, and, of course, *no hangovers*.

D. *WHAT TO DO THE DAY OF THE INTERVIEW*

Now comes the day of the interview itself. Give yourself plenty of time to get there. Plan to arrive somewhat ahead of the scheduled time, particularly if your appointment is in the fore part of the day. If a previous candidate fails to appear, the board might be ready for you a bit early. By early afternoon an oral board is almost invariably behind schedule if there are many candidates, and you may have to wait. Take along a book or magazine to read, or your application to review. But leave any extraneous material in the waiting room when you go in for your interview. In any event, relax and compose yourself.

The matter of dress is important. The board is forming impressions about you -- from your experience, your manners, your attitudes, and from your appearance. Give your personal appearance careful attention. Dress your *best*, but not your flashiest. Choose conservative, appropriate clothing, and be sure it and you are immaculate. This is a business interview, and your appearance should indicate that you regard it as such. Besides, being well-groomed and properly dressed will help boost your confidence.

Sooner or later, someone will call your name and escort you into the interview room. *This is it.* From here on you are on your own. It is too late for any more preparation. But, remember, you asked for this opportunity to prove your fitness, and you are here because your request was granted.

E. *WHAT HAPPENS WHEN YOU GO IN?*

The usual sequence of events will be as follows: The clerk (who is often the board stenographer) will introduce you to the chairman of the oral board, who will introduce you to each other member of the board. Acknowledge the introductions before you sit down. Do not be surprised if you find a microphone facing you or a stenotypist sitting by. Oral interviews are usually recorded, in the event of an appeal or other review.

Usually the chairman of the board will open the interview by reviewing the highlights of your education and work experience from your application -- primarily for the benefit of the other members of the board, as well as to get the material into the record. Do not interrupt or comment unless there is an error or significant misinterpretation; if so, do not hesitate. But do not quibble about insignificant matters. Usually, also, he will ask you some question about your education, your experience, or your present job -- partly to get you started talking, to establish the interviewing "rapport." He may start the actual questioning, or turn it over to one of the other members. Frequently each member undertakes the questioning on a particular area, one in which he is perhaps most competent. So you can expect each member to participate in the examination. And because the time is limited, you may expect some rather abrupt switches in the direction the questioning takes. Do not be upset by it. Normally, a board member will not pursue a single line of questioning unless he discovers a particular strength or weakness.

After each member has participated, the chairman will usually ask whether any member has any further questions, then will ask you if you have anything you wish to add. Unless you are expecting this question, it may floor you. Or worse, it may start you off on an extended, extemporaneous speech. The board is not usually seeking more information. The question is principally to offer you a last opportunity to present further qualifications or to indicate that you have nothing to add. So, if you feel that a significant qualification or characteristic has been overlooked, it is proper to point it out in a sentence or so. Do not compliment the board on the thoroughness of their examination -- they have been sketchy, and you know it. If you wish, merely say, "No thank you, I have nothing further to add." This is a point where you can "talk yourself out" of a good impression or fail to present an important bit of information. *Remember, you close the interview yourself.*

The chairman will then say,"That is all,Mr.Smith,thank you." Do not be startled; the interview is over, and quicker than you think. Say,"Thank you and good morning," gather up your belongings and take your leave. Save your sigh of relief for the other side of the door.

F. *HOW TO PUT YOUR BEST FOOT FORWARD*

Throughout all this process, you may feel that the board individually and collectively is trying to pierce your defenses, to seek out your hidden weaknesses, and to embarrass and confuse you. Actually, this is not true. They are obliged to make an appraisal of your qualifications for the job you are seeking, and they *want to see you in your best light*. Remember, they must interview all candidates and a noncooperative candidate may become a failure in spite of their best efforts to bring out his qualifications. Here are fifteen(15) suggestions that will help you:

1. Be Natural. Keep Your Attitude Confident,But Not Cocky

If *you* are not confident that you can do the job, do not expect the *board* to be. Do not apologize for your weaknesses, try to bring out your strong points. The board is interested in a positive, not a negative presentation. Cockiness will antagonize any board member, and make him wonder if you are covering up a weakness by a false show of strength.

2. Get Comfortable, But Don't Lounge or Sprawl

Sit erectly but not stiffly. A careless posture may lead the board to conclude you are careless in other things, or at least that you are not impressed by the importance of the occasion to you.Either conclusion is natural, even if incorrect. Do not fuss with your clothing, or with a pencil or an ashtray. Your hands may occasionally be useful to emphasize a point; do not let them become a point of distraction.

3. Do Not Wisecrack or Make Small Talk

This is a serious situation, and your attitude should show that you consider it as such. Further, the time of the board is limited; they do not want to waste it, and neither should you.

4. Do Not Exaggerate Your Experience or Abilities

In the first place, from information in the application,from other interviews and other sources, the board may know more about you than you think; in the second place, you probably will not get away with it in the first place. An experienced board is rather adept at spotting such a situation. Do not take the chance.

5. If You Know a Member of the Board, Do Not Make a Point of It, Yet Do Not Hide It.

Certainly you are not fooling him, and probably not the other members of the board. Do not try to take advantage of your acquaintanceship -- it will probably do you little good.

6. Do Not Dominate the Interview

Let the board do that. They will give you the clues -- do not assume that you have to do all the talking. Realize that the board has a number of questions to ask you, and do not try to take up all the interview time by showing off your extensive knowledge of the answer to the first one.

7. Be Attentive

You only have twenty minutes or so, and you should keep your attention at its sharpest throughout. When a member is addressing a problem or a question to you, give him your undivided attention. Address your reply principally to him, but do not exclude the other members of the board.

8. Do Not Interrupt

A board member may be stating a problem for you to analyze. He will ask you a question when the time comes. Let him state the problem, and wait for the question.

9. Make Sure You Understand the Question

Do not try to answer until you are sure what the question is. If it is not clear, restate it in your own words or ask the board member to clarify it for you. But do not haggle about minor elements.

10. Reply Promptly But Not Hastily

A common entry on oral board rating sheets is "candidate responded readily," or "candidate hesitated in replies." Respond as promptly and quickly as you can, but do not jump to a hasty, ill-considered answer.

11. Do Not Be Peremptory in Your Answers

A brief answer is proper -- but do not fire your answer back. That is a losing game from your point of view. The board member can probably ask questions much faster than you can answer them.

12. Do Not Try To Create the Answer You Think the Board Member Wants

He is interested in what kind of · mind you have and how it works -- not in playing games. Furthermore, he can usually spot this practice and will usually grade you down on it.

13. Do Not Switch Sides in Your Reply Merely to Agree With a Board Member

Frequently, a member will take a contrary position merely to draw you out and to see if you are willing and able to defend your point of view. Do not start a debate, yet do not surrender a good position. If a position is worth taking, it is worth defending.

1 Do Not Be Afraid to Admit an Error in Judgment if You Are Shown to Be Wrong

The board knows that you are forced to reply without any opportunity for careful consideration. Your answer may be demonstrably wrong. If so, admit it and get on with the interview.

15. Do Not Dwell at Length on Your Present Job

The opening question may relate to your present assignment. Answer the question but do not go into an extended discussion. You are being examined for a *new* job, not your present one. As a matter of fact, try to phrase *all* your answers in terms of the job for which you are being examined.

G. BASIS OF RATING

Probably you will forget most of these "do's" and "don'ts" when you walk into the oral interview room. Even remembering them all will not insure you a passing grade. Perhaps you did not have the qualifications in the first place. But remembering them *will* help you to put your best foot forward, without treading on the toes of the board members.

Rumor and popular opinion to the contrary notwithstanding, an oral board wants you to make the best appearance possible. They know you are under pressure -- but they also want to see how you respond to it as a guide to what your reaction would be under the pressures of the job you seek. They will be influenced by the degree of poise you display, the personal traits you show, and the manner in which you respond.

EXAMINATION SECTION

EXAMINATION SECTION
TEST 1

DIRECTIONS: Each question or incomplete statement is followed by several suggested answers or completions. Select the one that BEST answers the question or completes the statement. *PRINT THE LETTER OF THE CORRECT ANSWER IN THE SPACE AT THE RIGHT.*

1. When the abbreviation O.S. & Y. is mentioned in specifications, it is MOST probably in connection with the installation of
    A. electric motors   B. blowers
    C. valves   D. centrifugal pumps

1.___

2. Two inch *schedule 40* seamless steel pipe
    A. can contain a greater volume of fluid per lineal foot of pipe than 2 inch *schedule 80*
    B. has a much greater resistance to fluid flow than 2 inch *schedule 80*
    C. has only half the wall thickness of 2 inch *schedule 80*
    D. has approximately the same wall thickness as 4 inch standard, galvanized pipe

2.___

3. Roof drainage downspouts or leaders are sized according to
    A. type of building occupancy
    B. size of cold water risers
    C. type of connection to the sewer
    D. area of the horizontal projection of the drained area

3.___

4. An automatic sump pit pump maintains its prime by using a
    A. foot valve
    B. separate overhead tank of water
    C. float switch
    D. vacuum breaker

4.___

5. Sewage ejectors are used
    A. when there is insufficient water pressure to flush water closets
    B. when plumbing fixtures in the building are located below the level of the sewer in the street
    C. to carry boiler blow-off directly to the sewer
    D. to carry laboratory wastes to the sewer

5.___

6. A house trap is a device placed in the house drain immediately inside the foundation wall of the building. Its MAIN purpose is to
    A. prevent sewer gases from circulating in the building plumbing system
    B. provide a means for cleaning the waste lines of the plumbing system
    C. trap sediment flowing in the house drain to the street sewer
    D. maintain air pressure balance in the vent lines of the plumbing system

6.___

7. In plumbing, a stop-and-waste cock is GENERALLY used on 7.___
    A. gas supply mains
    B. waste or soil mains
    C. water supply lines subjected to low temperatures
    D. refrigerant lines connected to the refrigerant compressor

8. A tank discharges oil at the rate of 150 G.P.M. through a 8.___
4-inch I.D. pipe.
The velocity of flow, in fps, is MOST NEARLY
    A. 1.5   B. 2.4   C. 3.8   D. 7.6

9. Silver solder is often used 9.___
    A. to connect sections of cast iron sewer pipe
    B. to connect sections of copper tubing
    C. in place of welding rods when arc welding stainless
       steels
    D. for submerged arc welding of boiler drum seams

10. The ratio of the diameter of every vent stack to the 10.___
diameter of the soil or waste stack it serves MUST be
at least
    A. one-fourth   B. one-half
    C. three-fourths   D. one to one

11. The one of the following systems which would MOST likely 11.___
contain a *Plenum Chamber* is a(n) ____ system.
    A. steam heating   B. air distribution
    C. hot water heating   D. heating gas distribution

12. A wall composed of 12" of a material having a coefficient 12.___
of thermal conductivity (k) of 6 Btu (in.)/(hr.)(sq.ft.)
(deg.F), 3" of a material having (k) = 12, and 1" of a
material having (k) = 2, will have a thermal conductance (C),
neglecting film effects, in Btu/(hr)(sq.ft.)(deg.F) of
APPROXIMATELY
    A. 18   B. 14
    C. 1.15   D. none of the above

13. Two pounds of air are heated from 100°F to 300°F at 13.___
constant pressure.
The heat added to the air, in Btu, is MOST NEARLY
    A. 400   B. 160   C. 148   D. 96

14. 100 pounds per minute of outside air at 90°F dry bulb and 14.___
200 pounds per minute of recirculated air at 72°F dry bulb
are mixed in an air conditioning system.
The resulting dry bulb temperature will be, in °F, MOST
NEARLY
    A. 84   B. 78   C. 88   D. 81

15. In a compression refrigerating system, the principal 15.___
useful refrigerating effect is obtained in the
    A. condenser   B. evaporator
    C. expansion valve   D. compressor

16. Recirculation of conditioned air in an air conditioned building is done MAINLY to
    A. reduce refrigeration tonnage required
    B. increase room entropy
    C. increase air specific humidity
    D. reduce room temperature below the dewpoint
16.___

17. *Sweating* of cold water pipes in a room is due to the
    A. surface of the pipe being below the wet bulb temperature of the room air
    B. surface of the pipe being below the dewpoint temperature of the room air
    C. air in the room exceeding 100% relative humidity
    D. specific humidity exceeding the relative humidity
17.___

18. In a hot water heating system, one gallon of water per minute flowing through the radiator is cooled 30°F. The amount of heat in Btu's delivered by the water per gallon per hour is MOST NEARLY
    A. 250   B. 1500   C. 12500   D. 15000
18.___

19. In a two-stage air compressor, the intercooler is placed between the
    A. compressor and air receiver
    B. compressor and intake pipe
    C. after cooler and air receiver
    D. intake of the second stage and the discharge of the first stage
19.___

20. The quantity of heat required to change the state (e.g., liquid to vapor, or solid to liquid) of a body within a change in temperature is USUALLY called
    A. specific heat   B. enthalpy
    C. latent heat   D. entropy
20.___

21. A *unit* heater
    A. cannot use hot water inside its heating coils as the heating medium
    B. should never use a trap on the outlet line if steam is used for heating
    C. is usually equipped with a fan
    D. is usually not used in buildings having ceilings higher than 10 feet
21.___

22. When a refrigeration machine is in operation under normal load, the refrigerant leaving the compressor is in a state of
    A. low pressure vapor   B. hot liquid
    C. high pressure vapor   D. cold liquid
22.___

23. In a commercial ammonia refrigerating system, the ammonia that has just passed through the expansion valve
    A. is partially vaporized
    B. has become highly superheated
    C. has a greater enthalpy than it had before entering the expansion valve
    D. is all in a liquid state
23.___

24. Of the following constructions using bright aluminum foil, the one having the LOWEST value of heat conductivity at 50°F. is
    A. 3/8" air space faced one side with foil
    B. 1" air space faced both sides with foil
    C. 3/4" air space faced both sides with foil
    D. 3" air space divided into three 1" spaces by two curtains of foil

24.___

25. Evaporation is a _____ process.
    A. heating   B. mixing   C. reheating   D. cooling

25.___

KEY (CORRECT ANSWERS)

1. C		11. B	
2. A		12. D	
3. D		13. D	
4. A		14. B	
5. B		15. B	
6. A		16. A	
7. C		17. B	
8. C		18. D	
9. B		19. D	
10. B		20. C	

21. C
22. C
23. A
24. D
25. D

TEST 2

DIRECTIONS: Each question or incomplete statement is followed by several suggested answers or completions. Select the one that BEST answers the question or completes the statement. *PRINT THE LETTER OF THE CORRECT ANSWER IN THE SPACE AT THE RIGHT.*

1. The MOST common method of steam heating small buildings is the ____ system.   1.____
   - A. up-feed gravity two-pipe
   - B. up-feed gravity one-pipe
   - C. down-feed gravity one-pipe
   - D. down-feed gravity two-pipe

2. Whether the flow of fluid through a pipe is laminar or turbulent may be determined from the value of ____ number.   2.____
   - A. Rockwell's
   - B. Reynold's
   - C. Nussett's
   - D. Prandtl's

3. Of the following, the dividing point between the high pressure and low pressure side of a refrigeration system is the   3.____
   - A. evaporator
   - B. receiver
   - C. condenser
   - D. expansion valve

4. An 8-in. stone wall has 3/4-in. plaster on the inside. The overall heat transmission coefficient (U) of the wall is MOST NEARLY (fo = 6.0; stone thermal conductivity k = 12.5; thermal conductance of plaster C = 4.4; fi = 1.65)   4.____
   - A. 0.35
   - B. 0.45
   - C. 0.60
   - D. 0.75

5. The pressure relief valve in a hot water heating system is USUALLY connected to the   5.____
   - A. top of boiler
   - B. main header
   - C. expansion tank
   - D. highest radiator

6. A pitot tube inserted in a ventilating duct is USUALLY used to determine the ____ in the duct.   6.____
   - A. velocity pressure
   - B. total pressure
   - C. barometric pressure
   - D. static pressure in p.s.i. absolute

7. Wetness forming inside frame building walls is often due to water vapor migration into the wall. The vapor movement is usually from the warm air side to the cool air side. The vapor USUALLY moves in this direction because the   7.____
   - A. relative humidity of cool air is lower than the relative humidity of warm air
   - B. partial pressure of the vapor is lower on the cool side than on the warm air side of the wall

    C. warm air has a lower dewpoint temperature
    D. specific humidity or humidity ratio is so much
       lower for the warm air than for the cool air

8. An ice-making machine freezes 50 lbs. of water at 45°F.   8.__
to ice at 25°F. (under atmospheric conditions) in one hour.
The cooling load, in tons, of refrigeration is MOST NEARLY
    A. 0.7   B. 1.4   C. 6.8   D. 13.6

9. The pressure drop through a ventilating duct is 3.8 inches   9.__
of water when the air velocity is 32 feet per second.
The pressure drop, in inches of water, when the air velocity
is reduced to 24 feet per second will be MOST NEARLY
    A. 6.8   B. 3.8   C. 3.0   D. 2.1

10. The three methods in common use in the design and sizing   10.__
of air duct systems are known as
    A. abrupt enlargement, dynamic loss, maximum velocity
    B. turbulent loss, equal friction, static regain
    C. velocity reduction, equal friction, static regain
    D. velocity reduction, maximum velocity, dynamic loss

11. The actual amount of water vapor which atmospheric air   11.__
can hold is governed by the
    A. pressure   B. temperature
    C. relative humidity   D. specific volume

12. The aspect ratio in rectangular ducts, flues, or chimneys   12.__
is the ratio of the
    A. length to the diameter
    B. longer to the shorter side
    C. cross-section to the length
    D. cross-section to the diameter

13. When making the initial physical inspection of a new   13.__
installation of a multiple V-belt drive for an exhaust
fan, the MOST important item to check is the
    A. design calculations for the required number of belts
    B. lubrication of the motor bearings
    C. alignment of the pulleys
    D. tension of the belts

14. The quantity of heat, in Btu per hour, that a steam   14.__
radiator rated at 16 Edr will deliver is MOST NEARLY
    A. 1,600   B. 2,400   C. 3,800   D. 15,500

15. A compound gauge found in a steam line USUALLY shows   15.__
pressure
    A. in pounds per square inch and vacuum in inches of
       mercury
    B. and vacuum in pounds per square inch
    C. and vacuum in ounces per square inch
    D. and vacuum in inches of water

16. A dowel pin used in the assembly of machined parts   16.____
    A. fastens the parts together
    B. aligns the parts for assembly
    C. provides a hole for lubrication
    D. provides a means of handling the parts during assembly

17. Of the following types of fittings, the one that should   17.____
NOT be specified when writing specifications for gas
installations is the
    A. ground joint union   B. compression coupling
    C. gasketed union   D. right and left coupling

18. A manufacturer's data sheet may specify the minimum   18.____
diameter V-belt pulley which may be used on an electric
motor.
This is done to limit
    A. overheating
    B. the thrust load on the bearings
    C. the overhung load on the shaft
    D. the torsion in the shaft

19. A flat belt is used to transmit power to a fan. The force   19.____
transmitted by the belt is 44 pounds per inch of width.
The width of belt is 8 inches wide, and its velocity is
600 feet per minute.
The HP transmitted by the belt is MOST NEARLY
    A. 3   B. 4   C. 5   D. 6

20. Two meshing spur gears having 48 teeth and 80 teeth are   20.____
on shafts 8 inches apart.
The diametral pitch is
    A. 6   B. 8   C. 12   D. 16

21. In analyzing the acceleration of components of a machine,   21.____
the term *radius of gyration* is often used.
The units for this term would be
    A. ft-lb-sec^2 B. radians   C. ft^2 D. inches

22. A knurled finish would be specified where a   22.____
    A. smooth bearing surface is required
    B. leather drive belt is required to ride
    C. surface hardened condition is required
    D. hand gripping surface is required

23. A torque-wrench is used to tighten nuts on bolts or studs   23.____
when
    A. no lock-washer is used
    B. no wrench can be fitted to the bolt head
    C. the nut must be tighter than can be accomplished by hand
    D. the bolt is to be held to a predetermined stress limit

24. A tap drill is used to drill a hole so that an American   24.____
    Standard thread may be tapped in the material. A commercial
    tap is to be used so that the final fit will be a Class 2.
    The diameter of the hole made by the drill before tapping
    should be
    A. *equal* to the pitch diameter of the thread
    B. *slightly* larger than the root diameter of the tap
    C. *equal* to the root diameter of the tap
    D. *slightly* larger than the pitch diameter of the thread

25. A stud-bolt is   25.____
    A. a cylindrical bar threaded at both ends
    B. the former name of tap-bolts
    C. always required for tapped blind holes
    D. always used in the alignment of mating parts

KEY (CORRECT ANSWERS)

1. B		11. B	
2. B		12. B	
3. D		13. C	
4. C		14. C	
5. A		15. A	
6. A		16. B	
7. B		17. C	
8. A		18. C	
9. D		19. D	
10. C		20. B	

21. D
22. D
23. D
24. B
25. A

TEST 3

DIRECTIONS: Each question or incomplete statement is followed by several suggested answers or completions. Select the one that BEST answers the question or completes the statement. *PRINT THE LETTER OF THE CORRECT ANSWER IN THE SPACE AT THE RIGHT.*

1. The grout used in grouting a pump bedplate is USUALLY a mixture of
   A. neoprene and rubber
   B. cork and asphalt
   C. sand, cement, and water
   D. glass wool, plastic, and an accelerator

   1.____

2. After a centrifugal pump has been primed and started, the MAXIMUM safe suction lift, with all air leaks eliminated, is USUALLY ____ feet.
   A. 5   B. 15   C. 45   D. 60

   2.____

3. In a balanced draft steam power plant, the volume of flue gas (in cubic feet per minute) handled by the induced draft fan when compared to the volume of air (in cubic feet per minute) handled by the forced draft fan is
   A. smaller
   B. the same
   C. varies in accordance with the capacity of the plant
   D. greater

   3.____

4. Steam at 300 psia and 97% quality is discharged abruptly to the atmosphere.
   The steam immediately after discharge would
   A. precipitate to a saturated liquid
   B. decrease in moisture content
   C. gain in enthalpy
   D. expand to a lower pressure along a constant entropy process

   4.____

5. In the usual water tube boiler plant using coal under natural draft, the point where the maximum negative draft gage reading may be obtained is
   A. over the fire   B. at the top of the stack
   C. under the fire box   D. at the base of the stack

   5.____

6. An *unloader* in conjunction with an electrically driven air compressor
   A. starts and stops the motor
   B. prevents excessive air pressure from building up in the tank
   C. relieves the pressure on the compressor thus requiring a lower starting torque of the motor
   D. releases the air in case the motor overheats

   6.____

7. The heat content, in BTU, of 1 pound of steam at 150 psia   7.___
and 90% quality is MOST NEARLY (Note: Heat content of
liquid 330.5 BTU/#; Latent heat of vaporization 863.6 BTU/#)
    A. 1110   B. 1170   C. 1190   D. 1230

8. The indicated horsepower of a steam engine having a mean   8.___
indicated pressure of 110 psi, a stroke of 2 feet, an
effective piston area of 60 square inches, and 120 working
strokes per minute is MOST NEARLY
    A. 50   B. 40   C. 30   D. 20

9. In a forced circulation warm air heating system in a small   9.___
building, the blower is USUALLY instrumented so that the
blower
    A. starts when the burner starts
    B. stops when the air supplied to it drops to too low
       a temperature
    C. stops when the burner stops and only starts when the
       room temperature reaches a high enough value
    D. starts when the room thermostat shuts off the burner

10. If the efficiency of a boiler is 50%, the number of pounds   10.___
of coal of 13,000 Btu per pound heat content required to
change 10,000 pounds of water at 77°F. into steam at
212°F. in four hours is MOST NEARLY
    A. 650   B. 1300   C. 1700   D. 2550

11. Draft gauges are made with one leg inclined in order to   11.___
    A. expedite gage reading
    B. save wall space
    C. simplify instrument mounting
    D. increase the accuracy of the reading

12. The PRIMARY function of a feed-water heater in a steam   12.___
generating plant is to
    A. supply hot water to plumbing fixtures
    B. heat and condition water that is fed to the boiler
    C. generate hot water for hot water radiators
    D. provide make-up steam for high pressure steam systems

13. Electrostatic precipitrons are used for   13.___
    A. purification of water
    B. cleaning swimming pools
    C. cleaning flue gases of fine foreign particles
    D. purification of air for combustion in power plants

14. A by-pass loop in a piping system   14.___
    A. prevents excessive piping stressed by providing a
       method for expansion and contraction of piping due
       to temperature changes
    B. provides a method for increasing the capacity of
       the piping system
    C. tends to eliminate pulsations of fluid flow
    D. provides an emergency or secondary routing of fluid
       flow while the primary is shut down

15. A small boiler is to be hydrostatically tested at 100   15.___
    psig. The pressure may be generated by a pump or by a
    standpipe of water at 60°F.
    The required height of the water, in feet, in the stand-
    pipe would be MOST NEARLY
       A. 100   B. 230   C. 370   D. 491

16. The essential requirements for the smokeless combustion   16.___
    of fuels are
       A. time, pressure, volume
       B. time, temperature, turbulent flow
       C. temperature, volume, viscous flow
       D. time, pressure, viscous flow

17. Oil heaters are to be added at a particular installation.   17.___
    Originally, one heater was used delivering oil at 190°F.
    In the new installation, a total of four of the same
    heaters are to be used.
    If the outlet temperature is to remain at 190°F. but the
    quantity of oil is to be four times that of the original
    installation, the four heaters would MOST likely be piped up
       A. in series
       B. in parallel
       C. two in series and two in parallel
       D. two in series and two by-passed

18. When starting a large boiler unit using fuel oil, it is   18.___
    BEST to arrange the electrical controls so that the
       A. fuel oil is sprayed into the furnace and then the
          air supply is turned on
       B. fuel oil and air are turned on simultaneously
       C. air is turned on first
       D. oil is sprayed against the furnace wall to insure
          ignition before turning on the air

19. In a completely automatic rotary cup oil burning system,   19.___
    the
       A. burner operates continuously
       B. room thermostats operate the burner directly
       C. burner operation is controlled by steam pressure
       D. burner operation is controlled by oil pressure

20. A *haze* indicator would normally be found in a(n)   20.___
       A. fan room   B. air conditioning system
       C. water treatment plant   D. stack breeching

21. Sodium sulphite is commonly used in the treatment of   21.___
    feedwater for boilers.
    Its function is to
       A. prevent formation of scale
       B. acidify the water
       C. remove free oxygen from the water
       D. neutralize the water

22. Spalling of the refractory lining in the furnace of a steam boiler is MOST likely due to
    A. uneven heating and cooling within the refractory brick
    B. continuous overfiring of the boiler
    C. change in fuel from solid to liquid type
    D. slag accumulations on the furnace walls

22.___

23. When a flame failure occurs in an operating oil burner using number 6 oil, no attempt should be made to relight the burner without first
    A. checking the transformer connections
    B. adjusting the *Fyr-eye* safety switch to make sure the contacts are closed
    C. making sure the modulator operates at proper speed
    D. purging the unburned gases from the combustion chamber

23.___

24. The pressure at which #6 oil is delivered to a fully automatic rotary cup oil burner is controlled by adjusting the
    A. speed of the pump
    B. pressure relief valve on the return line
    C. inlet valve to the pump
    D. speed of the rotary cup

24.___

25. A pressure relief valve should be installed on the side of a pressure regulating valve in a pneumatic temperature control equipment system in order to prevent
    A. injury to the control equipment in case of failure of the pressure regulating valve
    B. reverse flow of air
    C. wire drawing in the circuit
    D. high temperatures of the air from damaging control equipment

25.___

KEY (CORRECT ANSWERS)

1. C		11. D	
2. B		12. B	
3. D		13. C	
4. B		14. D	
5. D		15. B	
6. C		16. B	
7. A		17. B	
8. A		18. C	
9. B		19. C	
10. C		20. D	

21. C
22. A
23. D
24. B
25. A

TEST 4

1. An engineer uses an Orsat apparatus to determine how efficiently a furnace is operating.
The measurement taken by this instrument is GENERALLY known as a _____ analysis.
   A. wet flue gas
   B. dry flue gas
   C. solids
   D. fuel

   1._____

2. In coal burning boilers, the air that enters the fire box under the grates is called _____ air.
   A. fresh   B. primary   C. secondary   D. cool

   2._____

3. In the combustion of the common fuels, the PRINCIPAL boiler heat loss is that due to the heat
   A. lost by incomplete combustion
   B. carried away by the moisture in the fuel
   C. lost by radiation
   D. carried away by the flue gases

   3._____

4. A water pH value of 7.0 at room temperature indicates
   A. neutrality
   B. active acidity
   C. active alkalinity
   D. turbulent flow

   4._____

5. The products of complete combustion of the simplest hydrocarbon gas, methane (CH_4) are
   A. CO and CH_8
   B. CO_2 and H_2
   C. CO_2 and H_2O
   D. CO and H_2O

   5._____

6. A single-phase motor takes 4 amperes at 120 volts. If the wattmeter reads 240 watts, the power factor is MOST NEARLY
   A. 0.5   B. 0.6   C. 0.7   D. 0.8

   6._____

7.

   7._____

An instrument circuit in a city department laboratory operates on 24 volts D.C. The circuit is wired as shown in the sketch above and contains instruments W, X, and Y. The current flowing through instrument X is _____ ampere(s).
   A. 1/2   B. 2   C. 4   D. 6

8. In a 3-phase, 4-wire electric supply system, the fourth   8.___
   wire is
   A. commonly known as the ground wire
   B. supplied in case of future additional electric loads
   C. used to reverse the direction (where necessary) of
      electric motors
   D. used specifically for the demand meter

9. Of the following, the device used to reduce the line   9.___
   voltages for use in bell and signal systems is the
   A. wheatstone bridge   B. transformer
   C. rheostat   D. potentiometer

10. In selecting a motor for hoisting operations, the MOST   10.___
    important consideration is the
    A. type of enclosure   B. maximum starting torque
    C. method of braking   D. method of speed control

11. Of the following single-phase electric motors, the one   11.___
    that will operate on either an A.C. or D.C. power supply
    is the ____ motor.
    A. repulsion   B. series
    C. split-phase   D. capacitor

12. The resistance of copper wire is 10.4 ohms per circular   12.___
    mil-foot.
    The approximate resistance of 500 feet of copper fixture
    wire whose diameter is 0.052 inches is MOST NEARLY ____ ohms.
    A. 8   B. 6   C. 4   D. 2

13. A sterilizer is marked 2000 watts, 120 volts.   13.___
    When connected to a 120-volt source, the resistance of
    the sterilizer, in ohms, is
    A. 5.2   B. 7.2   C. 14.4   D. 18.4

14. An A.C. induction motor of squirrel cage design GENERALLY 14.___
    develops its maximum torque at
    A. run-away speed   B. synchronous speed
    C. zero load   D. less than synchronous speed

15. An escalator whose mechanical drive is 80% efficient lifts 15.___
    2800 lbs. per minute a height of 16' for one hour. A D.C.
    motor, 85% efficient, drives this escalator.
    The heat liberated from this motor for one hour, in Btu, is
    MOST NEARLY
    A. 765   B. 1100   C. 1525   D. 1800

16. In the city, the MINIMUM distance between a steam pipe or 16.___
    hot water pipe and any woodwork or other combustible
    material is
    A. ½"   B. 1"   C. 2"   D. 3"

17. A cleanout chamber at the base of a chimney shall have   17.___
    a tight fitting metal door AT LEAST
       A. 4" x 4"   B. 8" x 8"   C. 18" x 18"   D. 24" x 24"

18. Locations and sizes of pipe chases or recesses in the walls 18.___
    of buildings in the city are subject to the control of the
       A. plumbing designer's discretion
       B. fire department regulations
       C. Building code of the city
       D. American Society of Mechanical Engineer's Code

19. The so-called *slenderness ratio* of a column is the ratio   19.___
    of its
       A. least moment of inertia to its unsupported length
       B. cross-section area to its length
       C. unsupported length to its least radius of gyration
       D. length of its minimum width

20. A 15" x 6" x 65# steel I beam has a sectional area of   20.___
    18.91 sq.in., a web thickness of 0.672, a moment of inertia
    about an axis through the center of gravity perpendicular
    to the web of 632.1 inches^4, and a radius of gyration about
    this axis of 5.78".
    Its section modulus about this axis is MOST NEARLY
       A. 940 inches^3 B. 110 inches^3
       C. 85 inches^3 D. 35 inches^2

21. A man is required to enter a compartment containing a   21.___
    high percentage of carbon dioxide gas.
    The apparatus that should be used is a(n)
       A. oxygen breathing apparatus
       B. air-tight suit
       C. filter mask
       D. mask containing a carbon black absorbent material

22. Accidents do not just happen.   22.___
    Of the following, the CHIEF implication of this statement
    for a supervisor is that
       A. accidents are sometimes deliberate
       B. an accident is the result of a combination of
          unavoidable circumstances
       C. he should fix individual blame for each accident
       D. he should give his employees training in accident
          prevention

23. A class C fire would be safely extinguished with a fire   23.___
    extinguisher containing
       A. carbon dioxide
       B. water
       C. carbon tetrachloride (pyrene)
       D. foam

24. Of the following, the SAFEST way to protect the domestic water supply from contamination by sewage or nonpotable water in the plumbing system is to provide   24.___
    A. double check valves
    B. swing connections
    C. air gaps
    D. tanks with overhead discharge

25. In modern passenger elevators, the car is prevented from starting before the door is closed and locked by means of   25.___
    A. a governor   B. limit switches
    C. wedge clamps   D. electrical interlocks

―――

KEY (CORRECT ANSWERS)

1. B		11. B	
2. B		12. D	
3. D		13. B	
4. A		14. D	
5. C		15. A	
6. A		16. A	
7. D		17. B	
8. A		18. C	
9. B		19. C	
10. B		20. C	

21. A
22. D
23. A
24. C
25. D

―――

EXAMINATION SECTION

DIRECTIONS: Each question or incomplete statement is followed by several suggested answers or completions. Select the one that BEST answers the question or completes the statement. *PRINT THE LETTER OF THE CORRECT ANSWER IN THE SPACE AT THE RIGHT.*

1. The combustion efficiency of a boiler can be determined   1.___
   with a CO_2 indicator and the
      A. under fire draft   B. boiler room humidity
      C. flue gas temperature   D. outside air temperature

2. A quick, practical method of determining if the cast-iron   2.___
   waste pipe delivered to a job has been damaged in transit
   is to
      A. hydraulically test it
      B. "ring" each length with a hammer
      C. drop each length to see whether it breaks
      D. visually examine the pipe for cracks

3. An electrostatic precipitator is used to   3.___
      A. filter the air supply
      B. remove sludge from the fuel oil
      C. remove particles from the fuel gas
      D. supply samples for an Orsat analysis

4. The PRIMARY cause of cracking and spalling of refractory   4.___
   lining in the furnace of a steam generator is *most likely*
   due to
      A. continuous over-firing of boiler
      B. slag accumulation on furnace walls
      C. change in fuel from solid to liquid
      D. uneven heating and cooling within the refractory brick

5. The term "effective temperature" in air conditioning means   5.___
      A. the dry bulb temperature
      B. the average of the wet and dry bulb temperatures
      C. the square root of the product of wet and dry
         bulb temperatures
      D. an arbitrary index combining the effects of temperature,
         humidity, and movement

6. The piping in all buildings having dual water distribution   6.___
   systems should be identified by a color coding of ____ for
   potable water lines and ____ for non-potable water lines.
      A. green; red   B. green; yellow
      C. yellow; green   D. yellow; red

7. The breaking of a component of a machine subjected to   7.___
   excessive vibration is called
      A. tensile failure   B. fatigue failure
      C. caustic embrittlement   D. amplitude failure

8. The TWO MOST important factors to be considered in
   selecting fans for ventilating systems are
   A. noise and efficiency
   B. space available and weight
   C. first cost and dimensional bulk
   D. construction and arrangement of drive

9. In the modern power plant deaerator, air is removed from
   water to
   A. reduce heat losses in the heaters
   B. reduce corrosion of boiler steel due to the air
   C. reduce the load of the main condenser air pumps
   D. prevent pumps from becoming vapor bound

10. The abbreviations BOD, COD, and DO are associated with
    A. flue gas analysis   B. air pollution control
    C. boiler water treatment   D. water pollution control

11. The piping of a newly installed drainage system should
    be tested upon completion of the rough plumbing with a
    head of water of NOT LESS THAN ____ feet.
    A. 10   B. 15   C. 20   D. 25

12. Of the following statements concerning aquastats, the
    one which is CORRECT is:
    A. Aquastats may be obtained with either a narrow or
       wide range of settings
    B. Aquastats have a mercury tube switch which is
       controlled by the stack switch
    C. An aquastat is a device used to shut down the burner
       in the event of low water in the boiler
    D. An aquastat should be located about 4 inches above
       the normal water line of the boiler

13. The SAFEST way to protect the domestic water supply from
    contamination by sewage or non-potable water is to insert
    A. air gaps
    B. swing connections
    C. double check valves
    D. tanks with overhead discharge

14. The MAIN function of a back-pressure valve which is some-
    times found in the connection between a water drain pipe
    and the sewer system is to
    A. equalize the pressure between the drain pipe and the
       sewer
    B. prevent sewer water from flowing into the drain pipe
    C. provide pressure to enable waste to reach the sewer
    D. make sure that there is not too much water pressure
       in the sewer line

15. Boiler water is neutral if its pH value is
    A. 0   B. 1   C. 7   D. 14

16. A domestic hot water mixing or tempering valve should be   16. ___
    preceded in the hot water line by a
    A. strainer   B. foot valve
    C. check valve   D. steam trap

17. Between a steam boiler and its safety valve there should   17. ___
    be
    A. no valve of any type
    B. a gate valve of the same size as the safety valve
    C. a swing check valve of at least the same size as
       the safety valve
    D. a cock having a clear opening equal in area to the
       pipe connecting the boiler and safety valve

18. A diagram of horizontal plumbing drainage lines should   18. ___
    have cleanouts shown
    A. at least every 25 feet
    B. at least every 100 feet
    C. wherever a basin is located
    D. wherever a change in direction occurs

19. When a Bourdon gauge is used to measure steam pressures,   19. ___
    some form of siphon or water seal must be maintained.
    The REASON for this is to
    A. obtain "absolute" pressure readings
    B. prevent steam from entering the gage
    C. prevent condensate from entering the gage
    D. obtain readings below atmospheric pressure

20. In a closed heat exchanger, oil is cooled by condensate   20. ___
    which is to be returned to a boiler. In order to avoid
    the possibility of contaminating the condensate with oil
    should a tube fail in the oil cooler, it would be GOOD
    practice to
    A. cool the oil by air instead of water
    B. treat the condensate with an oil solvent
    C. keep the oil pressure in the exchanger higher than
       the water pressure
    D. keep the water pressure in the exchanger higher than
       the oil pressure

21. A radiator thermostatic trap is used on a vacuum return   21. ___
    type of heating system to
    A. release the pocketed air only
    B. reduce the amount of condensate
    C. maintain a predetermined radiator water level
    D. prevent the return of live steam to the return line

22. According to the color coding of piping, fire protection   22. ___
    piping should be painted
    A. green   B. yellow   C. purple   D. red

23. The MAIN purpose of a standpipe system is to   23. ___
    A. supply the roof water tank
    B. provide water for firefighting
    C. circulate water for the heating system
    D. provide adequate pressure for the water supply

24. The name "Saybolt" is associated with the measurement of   24. ___
    A. viscosity   B. Btu content
    C. octane rating   D. temperature

25. Recirculation of conditioned air in an air-conditioned   25. ___
    building is done MAINLY to
    A. reduce refrigeration tonnage required
    B. increase room entrophy
    C. increase air specific humidity
    D. reduce room temperature below the dewpoint

26. In a plumbing installation, vent pipes are GENERALLY used   26. ___
    to
    A. prevent the loss of water seal from traps by
       evaporation
    B. prevent the loss of water seal due to several causes
       other than evaporation
    C. act as an additional path for liquids to flow through
       during normal use of a plumbing fixture
    D. prevent the backflow of water in a cross-connection
       between a drinking water line and a sewage line

27. The designation "150 W" cast on the bonnet of a gate   27. ___
    valve is an indication of the
    A. water working temperature
    B. water working pressure
    C. area of the opening in square inches
    D. weight of the valve in pounds

28. In the city, the size soil pipe necessary in a sewage   28. ___
    drainage system is determined by the
    A. legal occupancy of the building
    B. vertical height of the soil line
    C. number of restrooms connected to the soil line
    D. number of "fixture units" connected to the soil line

29. Fins or other extended surfaces are used on heat exchanger   29. ___
    tubes when
    A. the exchanger is a water-to-water exchanger
    B. water is on one side of the tube and condensing
       steam on the other side
    C. the surface coefficient of heat transfer on both
       sides of the tube is high
    D. the surface coefficient of heat transfer on one side
       of the tube is low compared to the coefficient on
       the other side of the tube

30. A fusible plug may be put in a fire tube boiler as an   30. ___
    emergency device to indicate low water level. The fusible
    plug is installed so that under normal operating conditions,
    A. both sides are exposed to steam
    B. one side is exposed to water and the other side to steam
    C. one side is exposed to steam and the other side to hot
       gases
    D. one side is exposed to the water and the other side
       to hot gases

31. Extra strong wrought-iron pipe, as compared to standard wrought-iron pipe of the same nominal size, has   31.____
    A. the same outside diameter but a smaller inside diameter
    B. the same inside diameter but a larger outside diameter
    C. a larger outside diameter and a smaller inside diameter
    D. larger inside and outside diameters

32. Fans may be rated on a dynamic or a static efficiency basis. The dynamic efficiency would *probably* be   32.____
    A. lower in value because of the energy absorbed by the air velocity
    B. the same as the static in the case of centrifugal blowers running at various speeds
    C. the same as the static in the case of axial flow blowers running at various speeds
    D. higher in value than the static

33. The function of the stack relay in an oil burner installation is to   33.____
    A. regulate the draft over the fire
    B. regulate the flow of fuel oil to the burner
    C. stop the motor if the oil has not ignited
    D. stop the motor if the water or steam pressure is too high

34. The type of centrifugal pump which is inherently balanced for hydraulic thrust is the   34.____
    A. double suction impeller type
    B. single suction impeller type
    C. single stage type
    D. multistage type

35. The specifications for a job using sheet lead calls for "4-lb. sheet lead."   35.____
    This means that each sheet should weigh
    A. 4 lbs.   B. 4 lbs. per square
    C. 4 lbs. per square foot   D. 4 lbs. per cubic inch

36. The total cooling load design conditions for a building are divided for convenience into two components. These are: 36.____
    A. infiltration and radiation
    B. sensible heat and latent heat
    C. wet and dry bulb temperatures
    D. solar heat gain and moisture transfer

37. The function of a Hartford loop used on some steam boilers is to   37.____
    A. limit boiler steam pressure
    B. limit temperature of the steam
    C. prevent high water levels in the boiler
    D. prevent back flow of water from the boiler into the return main

38. Vibration from a ventilating blower can be prevented from   38.___
being transmitted to the duct work by
    A. installing straighteners in the duct
    B. throttling the air supply to the blower
    C. bolting the blower tightly to the duct
    D. installing a canvas sleeve at the blower outlet

39. A specification states that access panels to suspended   39.___
ceiling will be of metal.
The MAIN reason for providing access panels is to
    A. improve the insulation of the ceiling
    B. improve the appearance of the ceiling
    C. make it easier to construct the building
    D. make it easier to maintain the building

40. A plumber on a job reports that the steamfitter has   40.___
installed a 3" steam line in a location at which the
plans show the house trap. On inspecting the job,
you should
    A. tell the steamfitter to remove the steam line
    B. study the condition to see if the house trap can
       be relocated
    C. tell the plumber and steamfitter to work it out
       between themselves and then report to you
    D. tell the plumber to find another location for the
       trap because the steamfitter has already completed
       his work

41. In the installation of any heating system, the MOST   41.___
important consideration is that
    A. all elements be made of a good grade of cast iron
    B. all radiators and connectors be mounted horizontally
    C. the smallest velocity of flow of heating medium be
       used
    D. there be proper clearance between hot surfaces and
       surrounding combustible material

42. Which one of the following is the PRIMARY object in   42.___
drawing up a set of specifications for materials to be
purchased?
    A. Control of quality
    B. Outline of intended use
    C. Establishment of standard sizes
    D. Location and method of inspection

43. The drawing which should be used as a LEGAL reference   43.___
when checking completed construction work is the ____
drawing.
    A. contract   B. assembly
    C. working or shop   D. preliminary

Questions 44-50.

DIRECTIONS: Questions 44 through 50 refer to the plumbing drawing
shown below.

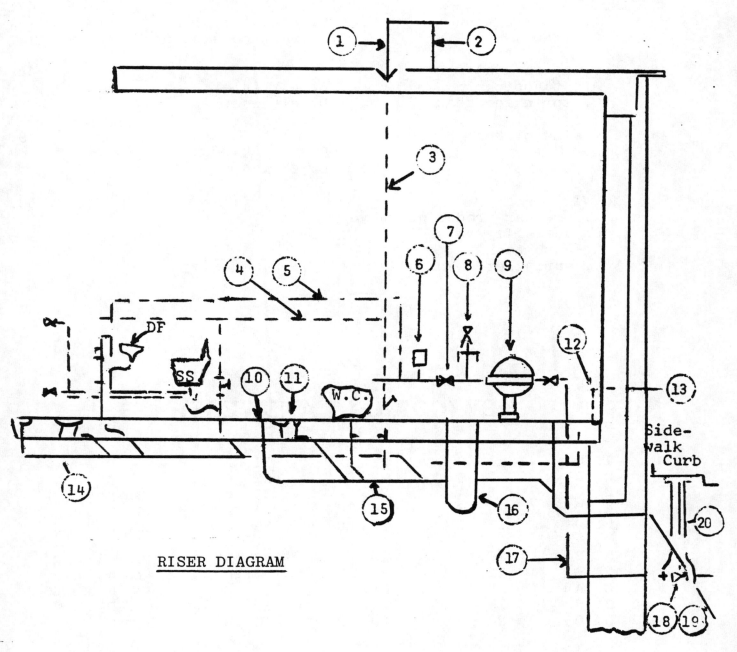

RISER DIAGRAM

44. According to the building code, the MINIMUM diameter of   44. ___
     No. ①and its minimum height, No. ②, respectively, are
         A. 2" and 12"   B. 3" and 18"
         C. 4" and 24"   D. 6" and 36"

45. No. ⑥ is a   45. ___
     , A. relief valve   B. shock absorber
         C. testing connection   D. drain

46. No. (9) is a
    A. strainer   B. float valve
    C. meter   D. pedestal

46. ___

47. No. (11) is a
    A. floor drain   B. cleanout
    C. trap   D. vent connection

47. ___

48. No. (13) is a(n)
    A. standpipe   B. air inlet
    C. sprinkler head   D. cleanout

48. ___

49. The size of No. (16) is
    A. 2" x 2"   B. 2" x 3"
    C. 3" x 3"   D. 4" x 4"

49. ___

50. No. (18) is a
    A. pressure reducing valve
    B. butterfly valve
    C. curb cock
    D. sprinkler head

50. ___

KEY (CORRECT ANSWERS)

1. C	11. A	21. D	31. A	41. D
2. B	12. C	22. D	32. D	42. A
3. C	13. A	23. B	33. C	43. A
4. D	14. B	24. A	34. A	44. C
5. D	15. C	25. A	35. C	45. B
6. B	16. A	26. B	36. B	46. C
7. B	17. A	27. B	37. D	47. A
8. A	18. D	28. D	38. D	48. B
9. B	19. B	29. D	39. D	49. D
10. D	20. D	30. D	40. B	50. C

EXAMINATION SECTION
TEST 1

DIRECTIONS: Each question or incomplete statement is followed by several suggested answers or completions. Select the one that BEST answers the question or completes the statement. *PRINT THE LETTER OF THE CORRECT ANSWER IN THE SPACE AT THE RIGHT.*

1. The capacity of a water-cooled condenser is LEAST affected by the   1.___
   A. surrounding air temperature
   B. water temperature
   C. refrigerant temperature
   D. quantity of water being circulated

2. The type of refrigeration system MOST commonly used in ice-skating rinks is the _____ system.   2.___
   A. direct expansion   B. simple secondary
   C. compound secondary   D. quadric resistance

3. The theoretical amount of refrigeration required to freeze one ton of water from 66°F to ice at 28°F in ONE day is _____ ton(s).   3.___
   A. 1.00   B. 1.25   C. 1.50   D. 1.75

4. The brine solution MOST commonly used in ice-skating rink piping, as a freezing medium, is a mixture of water and   4.___
   A. calcium chloride   B. sodium chloride
   C. glycol   D. methanol

5. In an absorption refrigeration system, latent heat is absorbed by the refrigerant in the   5.___
   A. evaporator and the generator
   B. evaporator and the absorber
   C. condenser and the absorber
   D. condenser and the generator

6. Of the following refrigerants, the one which has the HIGHEST evaporator pressure at the standard 5°F temperature is   6.___
   A. ammonia   B. freon 12
   C. methyl-chloride   D. carbon dioxide

7. The cooler in a refrigeration system that is equipped with automatic protective devices is MOST likely to be accidentally damaged by water freeze-up when the   7.___
   A. system is operating under reduced load
   B. system is operating at rated load
   C. system is being pumped down
   D. condenser cooling water flow is interrupted

8. The one of the following statements pertaining to
   refrigerant compressor lubricants that is NOT true is
   that
   A. the type of oil that is used to lubricate centrifugal
      compressors can also be used in speed increasers
   B. ammonia causes very little viscosity change in
      lubricating oil
   C. most reciprocating compressors handling ammonia or
      freons can be lubricated properly with an oil having
      a viscosity of 300 Sec. SU @ 100°F
   D. freon 12 causes very little viscosity change in
      lubricating oil

   8.___

9. The one of the following capacity controls which is
   USUALLY found in a refrigerant reciprocating-compressor
   system is a
   A. suction valve unloader
   B. throttling damper
   C. variable inlet guide vane
   D. condenser temperature control

   9.___

10. A thermostatic expansion valve is connected to an
    evaporator operating at 5°F and 11.8 psig. The valve
    is in equilibrium at 10° superheat, and the pressure in
    the bulb is 17.7 psig.
    The EQUIVALENT valve-spring pressure on the refrigerant
    side of the sensitive element is _____ psi.
    A. 5.9   B. 10.9   C. 22.8   D. 29.5

    10.___

11. A pressure gage on a compressed air tank reads 35.3 psi
    at 70°F.
    If, due to a fire, the temperature of the air in the
    tank were to increase to 600°F, the gage reading should
    be MOST NEARLY _____ psi.
    A. 70   B. 75   C. 80   D. 85

    11.___

12. An ADVANTAGE that variable-speed control of a fan has
    over damper control is
    A. lower first-cost of controls
    B. lower power consumption
    C. cheaper fan drive motor
    D. constant high efficiency throughout entire fan
       load range

    12.___

13. An intercooler is used on a two-stage air compressor to
    reduce the
    A. cylinder temperature in the first stage
    B. amount of condensate in the second stage
    C. back pressure of the air in the first stage
    D. work done on the air in the second stage

    13.___

14. Of the following, the BEST instrument to use to measure
    small pressure differentials at low pressure is the
    A. mercury manometer   B. bourdon tube gage
    C. pressurtrol   D. inclined manometer

    14.___

15. A modulating pressurtrol on a boiler should contain a   15.____
    A. potentiometer   B. mercury switch
    C. manual reset lever   D. level indicator

16. Of the following automatic refrigerant expansion valves,   16.____
    the one which can only be used in a system where the
    liquid refrigerant can largely be stored in the
    evaporator without danger of sending slugs of liquid
    refrigerant over to the compressor is the _____ valve.
    A. thermal-expansion   B. diaphragm-expansion
    C. high-side float   D. low-side float

17. The refrigerating effect of a fluid is measured by the   17.____
    amount of heat it is capable of absorbing from the time
    it enters the
    A. evaporator as a liquid and leaves as a vapor
    B. condenser as a vapor and leaves as a liquid
    C. expansion valve as a liquid and leaves as a vapor
    D. compressor as a vapor and leaves as a vapor

18. The one of the following which lists the refrigerants in   18.____
    CORRECT order of decreasing toxicity is:
    A. Ammonia, sulphur dioxide, freon 12
    B. Sulphur dioxide, ammonia, freon 12
    C. Sulphur dioxide, freon 12, ammonia
    D. Ammonia, freon 12, sulphur dioxide

19. The one of the following methods which would MOST likely   19.____
    be used to control the capacity of a large centrifugal
    refrigerant compressor is the _____ method.
    A. cylinder unloader
    B. variable cylinder clearance
    C. variable speed
    D. stop and start

20. On a hot summer day, the GREATEST number of people working   20.____
    in a large air-conditioned office would feel comfortable
    if the temperature and relative humidity were maintained
    at
    A. 77°F and 50%   B. 80°F and 60%
    C. 74°F and 30%   D. 71°F and 50%

21. The one of the following conditions which has the   21.____
    GREATEST effect on the suction pressure on a swimming
    pool circulating pump is a
    A. clogged hair and lint strainer
    B. loss of coagulant
    C. low pH level
    D. clogged filter

22. A coagulant used in swimming pool filters is   22.____
    A. alum   B. chlorine
    C. soda-ash   D. sodium hypochlorite

23. According to the health code, the pH reading of swimming   23.___
pool water should be between _____ and _____.
    A. 5.8; 6.4   B. 6.8; 7.4   C. 7.8; 8.4   D. 8.8; 9.4

24. An orthotolidine test is made to find out how much of   24.___
which substance is contained in a sample of water?
    A. Alum   B. Ammonia   C. Chlorine   D. Soda-ash

25. The MINIMUM air temperature which must be maintained in   25.___
an indoor swimming pool, except during the summer months,
is _____°F.
    A. 68   B. 71   C. 75   D. 82

———

KEY (CORRECT ANSWERS)

1. A		11. D	
2. B		12. B	
3. B		13. D	
4. A		14. D	
5. A		15. A	
6. D		16. C	
7. C		17. A	
8. D		18. B	
9. A		19. C	
10. A		20. A	

21. A
22. A
23. C
24. C
25. C

———

TEST 2

DIRECTIONS: Each question or incomplete statement is followed by several suggested answers or completions. Select the one that BEST answers the question or completes the statement. *PRINT THE LETTER OF THE CORRECT ANSWER IN THE SPACE AT THE RIGHT.*

1. A permit is required for the storage or use of liquid chlorine.
   This permit is issued by which city agency?
   The
   A. Health Services Administration
   B. Board of Standards and Appeals
   C. Board of Water Supply
   D. Fire Department

   1.___

2. The MINIMUM amount of free chlorine that swimming pool water should contain for proper disinfection is _____ part(s) per million.
   A. 1.0   B. 10   C. 40   D. 400

   2.___

3. The agency which approves gas masks suitable for use in high concentrations of chlorine gas is the United States
   A. Environmental Protection Agency
   B. Department of Agriculture
   C. Bureau of Mines
   D. Department of Defense

   3.___

4. The daily operational records of swimming pools which are required by the health code must be kept for a period of AT LEAST
   A. one month   B. six months
   C. one year   D. two years

   4.___

5. The one of the following which is NOT used as a filtering media in swimming pool filters is
   A. sand   B. quartz
   C. diatomaceous earth D. clay

   5.___

6. The point at which swimming pool filters should be backwashed is when the difference between the inlet and outlet pressure EXCEEDS _____ psi.
   A. 5   B. 10   C. 15   D. 20

   6.___

7. Of the following valves, the type which can be used to adjust the rate-of-flow in a swimming pool filter is the _____ valve.
   A. butterfly   B. needle
   C. gate   D. stop-and-waste

   7.___

8. When the coagulant in a swimming pool filter fails to jelly, the MOST likely cause of the failure is
   A. high water temperature
   B. excess bacteria in the water
   C. insufficient alkalinity of the water
   D. excess algae in the water

8.____

9. Of the following types of flow meters, the one that is MOST accurate is a
   A. concentric orifice
   B. venturi tube
   C. flow nozzle
   D. pitot tube

9.____

10. A spring pop safety valve on a fired high-pressure boiler fails to pop at its set pressure.
    Which of the following methods should be used to free the valve before retesting it?
    A. Strike the valve body with a soft lead hammer until it pops
    B. Raise the valve lifting-lever and release it
    C. Reduce the spring compression gradually until the valve opens
    D. Unscrew the valve one-quarter turn to relieve the strain on it

10.____

11. A device which retains the desired parts of a steam and water mixture while rejecting the undesired parts of the mixture is a
    A. check valve
    B. calorimeter
    C. stud tube
    D. steam trap

11.____

12. The PRIMARY purpose of using phosphate to treat boiler water is to
    A. precipitate the hardness constituents
    B. scavenge the dissolved oxygen
    C. dissolve the calcium
    D. dissolve the magnesium

12.____

13. The efficiency of a riveted joint is defined as the ratio of the
    A. plate thickness to the rivet diameter
    B. strength of the riveted joint to the strength of a welded joint
    C. strength of the riveted joint to the strength of the solid plate
    D. number of rivets in the first row of the joint to the total number of rivets on one side of the joint

13.____

14. A pump delivers 1500 pounds of water per minute against a total head of 200 feet.
    The water horsepower of this pump is MOST NEARLY
    A. 10   B. 40   C. 100   D. 600

14.____

15. A centrifugal water pump is direct-driven by a 25 HP   15.___
    900 RPM electric motor at rated load.
    In order to double the quantity of water delivered, it
    would be necessary to substitute a motor rated at
    _____ HP at _____ RPM.
        A. 40; 1200   B. 50; 1200   C. 100; 1800   D. 200; 1800

16. Of the following fire extinguisher ratings, the one   16.___
    which indicates that an extinguisher has the GREATEST
    capability for extinguishing wood, paper, and electrical
    fires is
        A. 2-A:16-B:C   B. 4-A:4-B:C
        C. 16-A   D. 8-B

17. Of the following combinations of oil burners and fuel   17.___
    oils, the combination which is the MOST hazardous to
    fire-up when placing a cold boiler into service is the
        A. compressed air-atomized burner firing light oil
        B. steam-atomized burner firing heavy oil
        C. air-atomized burner firing heavy oil
        D. mechanically-atomized burner firing heavy oil

18. It is usually desirable to have a program which will   18.___
    create and maintain the interest of workers in safety.
    Of the following, the one which such a program CANNOT
    do is to
        A. develop safe work habits
        B. compensate for unsafe procedures
        C. provide a channel of communications between workers
           and management
        D. give employees a chance to participate in accident
           prevention activities

19. Because of a ruptured ammonia tank, the concentration of 19.___
    ammonia gas in a room exceeds 3%.
    The wearing of a gas mask, as the only protective device,
    by a person entering the room is
        A. *recommended*, because the gas mask alone is suffi-
           cient protection
        B. *not recommended*, because the ammonia will severely
           irritate the skin
        C. *not recommended*, because the gas mask is not effec-
           tive at concentrations above 3%
        D. *not recommended*, because ammonia is flammable

20. The Occupational Safety and Health Act of 1970 provided   20.___
    for
        A. penalties against employees for safety violations
        B. complete occupational safety against all hazards
        C. standards of employee discipline
        D. employees' right to review a copy of a safety
           citation against the employer

21. An aftercooler on a reciprocating air compressor is used   21.___
    PRIMARILY to
        A. increase compressor capacity
        B. improve compressor efficiency
        C. condense the moisture in the compressed air
        D. cool the lubricating oil

22. The one of the following tasks which is an example of   22.___
    preventive maintenance is
        A. replacing a leaking water pipe nipple
        B. cleaning the cup on a rotary cup burner
        C. cleaning a completely clogged oil strainer
        D. replacing a blown fuse

23. The four MAIN causes of failure of three-phase electric   23.___
    motors are
        A. dirt, friction, moisture, single-phasing
        B. friction, moisture, single-phasing, vibration
        C. dirt, moisture, single-phasing, vibration
        D. dirt, friction, moisture, vibration

24. The one of the following electrical control components   24.___
    that may be lubricated is the
        A. drum controller's copper-to-copper contacts
        B. relay bearing
        C. starter silver contact
        D. shunt spring

25. In the planning of a preventive maintenance program, the   25.___
    FIRST requirement is to
        A. prepare a maintenance manual
        B. inventory the equipment
        C. inventory the tools available
        D. prepare repair requisitions for all equipment not
           operating satisfactorily

KEY (CORRECT ANSWERS)

1. D	11. D
2. A	12. A
3. C	13. C
4. B	14. A
5. D	15. D
6. B	16. B
7. A	17. D
8. C	18. B
9. B	19. B
10. B	20. D

21. C
22. B
23. D
24. A
25. B

EXAMINATION SECTION
TEST 1

DIRECTIONS: Each question or incomplete statement is followed by several suggested answers or completions. Select the one that BEST answers the question or completes the statement. *PRINT THE LETTER OF THE CORRECT ANSWER IN THE SPACE AT THE RIGHT.*

1. The MAIN function of a *steam separator* in a steam power plant is to
   A. reduce steam pressure
   B. remove excess oil vapors from the steam
   C. increase steam quality
   D. reduce back-pressure on the steam-driven equipment

   1.___

2. The MAIN purpose of a *dip tube* in a low-pressure hot water system is to
   A. prevent air from entering the main
   B. determine the level of water in the boiler
   C. reduce air pollution
   D. eliminate condensation when starting up

   2.___

3. The rating of a unit ventilator is USUALLY determined by a(n)
   A. anemometer   B. hydrometer
   C. psychrometer   D. ammeter

   3.___

4. Of the following devices, the one that is used to record the air-flow-steam-flow relationship of a boiler in a steam plant is a
   A. Orsat analyzer   B. manometer
   C. steam-flow meter   D. heat meter

   4.___

5. Of the following types of gas fuels, the one which has the HIGHEST BTU content per cubic foot is _____ gas.
   A. manufactured   B. coke-oven
   C. liquid petroleum   D. natural

   5.___

6. Of the following gasket materials, the one which is BEST to use when oil at 300°F is being carried in a pipe is
   A. fiber and paper   B. synthetic rubber
   C. asbestos composition   D. corrugated copper

   6.___

7. A monolithic repair of a slightly damaged sectional magnesia insulation covering is BEST made by
   A. wiring in a *Dutchman* and filling the voids with magnesia cement
   B. covering the damaged area with asbestos laminations
   C. filling in the broken portion with glass-fiber insulating cement
   D. replacing the entire section

   7.___

8. Of the following piping materials, the one that should
   NOT be used in a fuel-oil piping system is
      A. galvanized iron   B. type K copper tubing
      C. brass pipe   D. steel pipe

   8.___

9. A valve is marked *300 WOG*.
   This valve could NOT be properly used in a pipe conveying
   _____ pounds gage maximum.
      A. oil at 300   B. air at 100
      C. water at 150   D. steam at 300

   9.___

10. A steam gage connection for a large boiler is connected
    to the top of the water column and is then brought down
    to the operating level 24 feet below. The gage actually
    reads 605 psi.
    The ACTUAL gage pressure in the boiler is MOST NEARLY
    _____ psi.
       A. 590   B. 595   C. 610   D. 620

    10.___

11. Of the following types of industrial oil burners, the
    one that is COMPLETELY adaptable to fully automatic
    operation or wide variations in firing rate is the
    _____ burner.
       A. mechanical-pressure type
       B. air-atomizing
       C. steam-atomizing
       D. horizontal rotary-cup

    11.___

12. A full backward curve type centrifugal fan is being used
    in a coal-fired power plant for forced draft. Assume
    that after adjusting the speed of the fan, it is still
    too high, resulting in more pressure than is necessary
    to overcome the resistance of the fuel bed and boiler.
    To correct this situation, it would be BEST to replace
    the fan with one of a _____ diameter, running at _____
    rpm and with a _____ wheel.
       A. *smaller*; greater; wider
       B. *larger*; less; wider
       C. *larger*; greater; smaller
       D. *smaller*; less; smaller

    12.___

13. Short stroking in a steam-driven reciprocating pump
    results in both a(n) _____ in steam consumption and a(n)
    _____ in pumping capacity.
       A. *decrease*; decrease   B. *increase*; increase
       C. *decrease*; increase   D. *increase*; decrease

    13.___

14. Caustic embrittlement is the weakening of boiler steel
    as the result of inner crystalline cracks.
    This condition is caused by BOTH long exposure to
       A. a combination of stress and highly acidic water
       B. stress in the presence of free oxygen and highly
          acidic water
       C. a combination of stress and water with a pH of 7
       D. a combination of stress and highly alkaline water

    14.___

15. Of the following statements pertaining to feedwater   15.___
    injectors, the one which is MOST nearly correct is that
    the injectors
    A. are very efficient pumping units
    B. are practical only on small boilers
    C. are very reliable in operation on all types of
       boilers
    D. can handle 250 to 300 degree water

16. In reference to power plant pumps, the letters N.P.S.H.   16.___
    are an abbreviation for
    A. Non Positive Static Head
    B. Net Position Static Head
    C. Non Positive Standard Head
    D. Net Positive Suction Head

17. A pump's maintenance is based on a preventive maintenance 17.___
    schedule.
    This means that the schedule should GENERALLY be deter-
    mined by the
    A. actual time lapse between maintenance checks
    B. actual number of pump-operating hours
    C. pump's actual operating performance
    D. operating performance of the equipment connected to
       the pump

18. Periodic inspection and testing of mechanical equipment   18.___
    by the staff at a plant is done MAINLY to
    A. help the men to better understand the operation of
       the equipment
    B. keep the men busy during slack times
    C. encourage the men to better understand each others'
       working capabilities
    D. discover minor equipment faults before they develop
       into major breakdowns

19. In planning a preventive maintenance program, the FIRST   19.___
    step to be taken is to
    A. repair all equipment that is not in service
    B. check all fuel oil burner tips
    C. make an inventory of all plant equipment
    D. check all electrical wiring to motors

20. An electric motor having class A insulation has been   20.___
    permitted to operate continuously at rated load even
    though the internal insulation temperature reads 10°C
    above the allowable maximum internal temperature.
    Operating at this excessive temperature WOULD
    A. require frequent lubrication of the motor bearings
    B. reduce the life expectancy of the electric motor
    C. require an increase in voltage
    D. reduce the power factor to one-half of its normal
       value

21. The synchronous speed of a three-phase squirrel cage induction motor operating from a fixed frequency system can ONLY be changed by altering the
    A. rated locked-rotor torque
    B. rheostat position of the unloaded machine
    C. brush holder position
    D. number of poles in the stator
21.___

22. A thermal overload relay on an electric motor has been frequently tripping out.
    Of the following actions, the BEST one to take first to correct this problem would be to
    A. bypass the relay
    B. block the relay on a closed position
    C. clean the relay contacts
    D. arbitrarily readjust the relay setting
22.___

23. An air heater for a steam generator providing combustion air at temperatures ranging upward from 300°F will often effect savings in fuel ranging from
    A. 1 to 3%   B. 5 to 10%   C. 12 to 15%   D. 17 to 20%
23.___

24. You have been asked to make an inspection of the super-heater of a steam generator for external corrosion.
    You should be aware that if the direction of gas flow perpendicular to a tangent to the superheater tube is considered to be the 12 o'clock position, the GREATEST metal loss due to external corrosion usually occurs on the _____ o'clock and _____ o'clock sectors of the tube.
    A. 12; 6   B. 10; 2   C. 8; 3   D. 7; 5
24.___

25. In the steam generating plant to which you are assigned, the starting-up time and the shutting-down time for the boiler is determined by the time required to limit the thermal stresses in the drums and headers. The drums and headers have rolled tube joints.
    The temperature change in saturated temperature per hour for limit controlled heating and cooling rates for this boiler is established at _____ change.
    A. 50°F   B. 75°F   C. 100°F   D. 200°F
25.___

KEY (CORRECT ANSWERS)

1. C	6. C	11. D	16. D	21. D
2. A	7. A	12. B	17. B	22. C
3. A	8. A	13. D	18. D	23. B
4. C	9. D	14. D	19. C	24. B
5. C	10. B	15. B	20. B	25. C

TEST 2

Each question or incomplete statement is followed by several suggested answers or completions. Select the one that BEST answers the question or completes the statement. *PRINT THE LETTER OF THE CORRECT ANSWER IN THE SPACE AT THE RIGHT.*

1. Assume that the optimum pH level of boiler feedwater for a boiler installation ranges between 8.0 and 9.5. The alkalizer used in the feedwater treatment to maintain this optimum pH level SHOULD introduce
    A. an average amount of iron and copper corrosion products into the steam cycle
    B. an increase of partial pressure of the carbon dioxide in the steam
    C. the least amount of iron and copper corrosion products into the boiler cycle
    D. a control of corrosion rates by forming a coating on the surfaces contacted by the steam

1.____

2. The ppm of sodium sulfite that can be *safely* used for the chemical scavenging of oxygen in boiler feedwater is DEPENDENT upon the
    A. steam output of the boiler
    B. boiler operating pressure
    C. number of boiler steam drums
    D. construction of the boiler

2.____

3. Of the following piping materials, the one which is NOT generally used for pneumatic temperature control systems is
    A. copper   B. plastic
    C. steel   D. galvanized iron

3.____

4. In accordance with recommended maintenance practice, thermostats used in a pneumatic temperature control system SHOULD be checked
    A. weekly   B. bi-monthly
    C. monthly   D. once a year

4.____

5. Of the following, the BEST method to use to determine the moisture level in a refrigeration system is to
    A. weigh the drier after it has been in the system for a period of time
    B. visually check the sight glass for particles of corrosion
    C. use a moisture indicator
    D. test a sample of lubricating oil with phosphorus pentoxide

5.____

6. A full-flow drier is USUALLY recommended to be used in a   6.___
   hermetic refrigeration compressor system to keep the
   system dry and to
   A. prevent the products of decomposition from getting
      into the evaporator in the event of a motor burn-out
   B. condense cut liquid refrigerant during compressor
      off cycles and compressor start-up
   C. prevent the compressor unit from decreasing in
      capacity
   D. prevent the liquid from dumping into the compressor
      crankcase

7. An economizer in a steam boiler is used to raise the   7.___
   temperature of the
   A. combustion air for firing fuel oil utilizing some
      of the heat in the exit flue gases
   B. combustion air for firing fuel oil utilizing some
      of the heat in the exhaust steam from the turbines
      of steam engines
   C. boiler feedwater by utilizing some of the heat in
      the exit flue gases
   D. boiler feedwater by utilizing some of the heat in
      the exhaust steam from the turbines or steam engines

8. A mixed-base grease is a grease that is prepared by mixing   8.___
   lubricating oil with
   A. one metallic soap   B. two metallic soaps
   C. a synthetic lubricant   D. heavy gear oil

9. Of the following lubricants, the one which is classified   9.___
   as a circulating oil is _____ oil.
   A. turbine   B. gear
   C. machine   D. steam-cylinder

10. You are supervising the installation of a steam-driven   10.___
    reciprocating pump. The pump's air chamber is missing
    and you have to replace it with one with several salvaged
    ones.
    The salvaged air chamber selected should have a volume
    equal to MOST NEARLY _____ the piston displacement of
    the pump.
    A. half of   B. $1\frac{1}{2}$ times
    C. 2 times   D. $2\frac{1}{2}$ times

11. Economical partial-load operation of steam turbines is   11.___
    obtained by minimizing throttling losses.
    This is accomplished by
    A. reducing the boiler pressure and temperature
    B. throttling the steam flow into the uncontrolled
       set of nozzles
    C. dividing the first-stage nozzles into several groups
       and providing a steam control valve for each group
    D. controlling the fuel flow to the steam generator

12. You are ordering two pump wearing rings for a centrifugal   12.___
    pump.
    These rings are GENERALLY identified as
       A. two wearing rings
       B. one drive wearing ring and one casing wearing ring
       C. one casing wearing ring and one impeller wearing ring
       D. one first-stage wearing ring and one drive wearing
          ring

13. A thermo-hydraulic feedwater regulator is used to   13.___
    regulate the flow of water to a drum-type boiler.
    The amount of water input to the boiler is controlled
    in proportion to the
       A. boiler load
       B. setting of the feed pump relief valve
       C. amount of water in the outer tube that flashes into
          steam
       D. water level in the drum

14. The standard capacity rating conditions for any refriger- 14.___
    ation compressor is _____ psig for the suction and _____
    psig for the discharge.
       A. 5°F, 19.6; 86°F, 154.5   B. 5°F, 9.6; 96°F, 154.5
       C. 10°F, 9.6; 96°F, 144.5   D. 10°F, 19.6; 96°F, 134.5

15. Of the following, the MAIN purpose of a subcooler in a   15.___
    refrigerant piping system for a two-stage system is to
       A. reduce the total power requirements and total heat
          rejection to the second stage
       B. reduce total power requirements and return oil to
          the compressor
       C. improve the flow of evaporator gas per ton and
          increase the temperature
       D. increase the heat rejection per ton and avoid system
          shutdown

16. In large refrigeration systems, the USUAL location for   16.___
    charging the refrigeration system is into the
       A. suction line
       B. liquid line between the receiver shut-off valve
          and the expansion valve
       C. line between the condenser and the compressor
       D. line between the high pressure cut-off switch and
          the expansion valve

17. The effect of a voltage variation to 90 percent of normal 17.___
    voltage, for a compound wound DC motor, on the FULL load
    current is
       A. an increase in the full load current of approximate-
          ly 10%
       B. a decrease in the full load current of approximately
          10%
       C. zero
       D. a decrease in the full load current 20%

18. The purpose of a current-limiting reactor is to place an   18.___
    upper limit on the available short-circuit current that
    can occur under fault conditions.
    The reactor accomplishes this by contributing _____ to
    the circuit.
    A. additional capacitance
    B. reduced inductive reactance
    C. reduced capacitance
    D. additional inductive reactance

19. Alternating current electric motors are usually guaran-   19.___
    teed to operate satisfactorily and to deliver their full
    horsepower PROVIDED the electrical power delivered to
    the motor is at the rated
    A. voltage and at plus or minus 5 percent frequency
       variation
    B. frequency and at a voltage 15 percent above or
       below rating
    C. voltage and at plus or minus 10 percent frequency
       variation
    D. frequency and at a voltage 20 percent above or
       below rating

20. A three-phase AC motor is connected to a 230 volt, three-   20.___
    phase, alternating current line. With this motor running
    at full load, the line current is found to be 20 amperes,
    with a power factor of 0.75.
    Under these conditions, the power, in kilowatts, supplied
    to this motor will be MOST NEARLY
    A. 3.5   B. 6.0   C. 10.5   D. 18.0

21. In accordance with the air pollution control code, no   21.___
    person shall cause or permit the emission of air
    contaminants from a boiler with a capacity of 500 million
    BTU per hour or more, if the air contaminant emitted has
    a sulfur dioxide content of MORE than _____ parts per
    million by volume of undiluted emissions measured at
    _____ percent excess air.
    A. 300; 15   B. 200; 10   C. 200; 15   D. 300; 10

22. Of the following statements concerning the requirements   22.___
    of the air pollution control code, the one which is the
    MOST complete and correct is that the owner of equipment
    A. and apparatus shall maintain such equipment and appa-
       ratus in good operating order by regular inspection
       and cleaning and by promptly making repairs
    B. shall maintain the equipment in good operating condi-
       tion by making inspections and repairs on a regular
       basis
    C. and apparatus shall maintain the equipment and
       apparatus in operating condition by regular inspec-
       tion and cleaning
    D. shall maintain such equipment in good working order
       by regular inspection and cleaning and by making
       repairs on a scheduled basis

23. Assume that one of your assistants was near the Freon 11 refrigeration system when a liquid Freon line ruptured. Some of the liquid Freon 11 has gotten into your assistant's right eye.
Of the following actions, the one which you should NOT take is to
    A. immediately call for an eye specialist (medical doctor)
    B. gently and quickly rub the Freon 11 out of the eye
    C. use a boric-acid solution to clean out the Freon 11 from his eye
    D. wash the eye by gently blowing the Freon 11 out of his eye with air

23.___

24. Assume that a fire breaks out in an electrical control panel board.
Of the following types of portable fire extinguishers, the BEST one to use to put out this fire would be a _____ type.
    A. dry-chemical   B. soda-acid
    C. foam   D. water-stream

24.___

25. Assume that you are checking the water level in a boiler which is on the line in a power plant. Upon opening the gage cocks, you determine that the water level was above the top gage cock.
Of the following actions, the BEST one to take FIRST in this situation would be to
    A. shut off the fuel and air supply
    B. surface-blow the boiler
    C. close the steam-outlet valve from the boiler
    D. increase the speed of the feedwater pump

25.___

KEY (CORRECT ANSWERS)

1. C		11. C	
2. B		12. C	
3. C		13. D	
4. D		14. A	
5. C		15. A	
6. A		16. B	
7. C		17. A	
8. B		18. D	
9. A		19. A	
10. D		20. B	

21. B
22. A
23. B
24. A
25. C

EXAMINATION SECTION
TEST 1

DIRECTIONS: Each question or incomplete statement is followed by
several suggested answers or completions. Select the
one that BEST answers the question or completes the
statement. *PRINT THE LETTER OF THE CORRECT ANSWER IN
THE SPACE AT THE RIGHT.*

1. Asbestos is used as a covering on electrical wires to   1.___
   provide protection from
   A. high voltage   B. high temperatures
   C. water damage   D. electrolysis

2. The rating term *240 volts, 10 H.P.* would be *properly* used   2.___
   to describe a
   A. transformer   B. storage battery
   C. motor   D. rectifier

3. Rigid steel conduit used for the protection of electrical   3.___
   wiring is *generally* either galvanized or enameled both
   inside and out in order to
   A. prevent damage to the wire insulation
   B. make threading of the conduit easier
   C. prevent corrosion of the conduit
   D. make the conduit easier to handle

4. BX is *commonly* used to indicate   4.___
   A. rigid conduit without wires
   B. flexible conduit without wires
   C. insulated wires covered with flexible steel armor
   D. insulated wires covered with a non-metallic covering

5. If a test lamp does not light when placed in series with   5.___
   a fuse and an appropriate battery, it is a *good* indication
   that the fuse
   A. is open-circuited
   B. is short-circuited
   C. is in operating condition
   D. has zero resistance

6. Of the following, the SIMPLEST wood joint to make is a   6.___
   A. half lap joint   B. mortise and tenon
   C. butt joint   D. multiple dovetail

7. To accurately cut a number of lengths of wood at an angle   7.___
   of 45 degrees, it would be BEST to use a
   A. protractor   B. mitre-box
   C. triangle   D. square

8. The soffit of a beam is the   8.___
   A. span   B. side   C. bottom   D. top

9. A nail set is a tool used for
    A. straightening bent nails
    B. cutting nails to specified size
    C. sinking a nail head in wood
    D. measuring nail size

10. It is unlawful in the city to
    A. use wooden lath
    B. have ceiling lath run in one direction only
    C. break joints when using wood lath
    D. run wood lath through from room to room

11. A concrete mix for a construction job requires a certain
    ratio of cement, water, sand, and small stones.
    The MOST serious error in mixing would be to use 20% too
    much
    A. sand   B. water
    C. small stones   D. mixing time

12. Impurities in a mortar which may seriously affect its
    strength are MOST likely to enter the mortar with the
    A. mixing water   B. sand
    C. lime   D. gypsum

13. One *advantage* of using plywood instead of boards for
    concrete forms is that plywood
    A. needs no bracing
    B. does not split easily
    C. sticks less to concrete
    D. insulates concrete against freezing

14. Concrete will crack MOST easily when it is subject to
    A. compression   B. bearing
    C. bonding   D. tension

15. Where a smooth dense finish is desired for a concrete
    surface, it will BEST be produced by using a
    A. wood float   B. level
    C. steel trowel   D. vibrator

16. Sewer gas is prevented from backing up through a fixture
    by a
    A. water trap   B. vent pipe
    C. check valve   D. float valve

17. Packing is used in an adjustable water valve MAINLY to
    A. make it air-tight
    B. prevent mechanical wear
    C. regulate the water pressure
    D. make it water-tight

9.__

10.__

11.__

12.__

13.__

14.__

15.__

16.__

17.

18. Good practice requires that the end of a piece of water pipe be reamed to remove the inside burr after it has been cut to length.
The purpose of the reaming is to
   A. finish the pipe accurately to length
   B. make the threading easier
   C. avoid cutting of the workers' hands
   D. allow free passage for the flow of water

18.___

19. The MAIN reason for pitching a steam pipe in a heating system is to
   A. prevent accumulation of condensed steam
   B. present a smaller radiating surface
   C. facilitate repairs
   D. reduce friction in the pipe

19.___

20. When fitting pipe together, poor alignment of pipe and fittings would MOST likely result in
   A. leaky joints
   B. cracking of the pipe on expansion
   C. formation of hot spots
   D. cracking of the pipe on contraction

20.___

_____

KEY (CORRECT ANSWERS)

1. B		11. B	
2. C		12. B	
3. C		13. B	
4. C		14. D	
5. A		15. C	
6. C		16. A	
7. B		17. D	
8. C		18. D	
9. C		19. A	
10. D		20. A	

_____

TEST 2

DIRECTIONS: Each question or incomplete statement is followed by several suggested answers or completions. Select the one that BEST answers the question or completes the statement. *PRINT THE LETTER OF THE CORRECT ANSWER IN THE SPACE AT THE RIGHT.*

1. Roofing nails are *generally*   1.__
    A. brass plated   B. galvanized
    C. cement coated   D. nickel plated

2. Specifications for a roofing job call for *3 lb. sheet lead.*   2.__
This means that each sheet should weigh 3 lbs. per
    A. square inch   B. square foot
    C. square yard   D. sheet

3. The MAIN reason for using flashing at the intersection of   3.__
different roof planes is to
    A. increase the durability of the shingles
    B. simplify the installation of the shingles
    C. waterproof the roof
    D. improve the appearance of the roof

4. Of the following roofing materials, the one that is MOST   4.__
frequently used in *built-up* roofs is
    A. asbestos shingles   B. three-ply felt
    C. sheet copper   D. wood sheathing

5. As used in roofing, a *square* refers to   5.__
    A. a tool for lining up the roofing with the eaves of
       the house
    B. one hundred square feet of roofing
    C. one hundred shingles of roofing
    D. one hundred pounds of roofing

6. In the process of replacing a pane of window glass, the   6.__
old putty should be scraped off the window sash and the
wood surfaces then primed with
    A. resin oil   B. shellac
    C. linseed oil   D. enamel

7. The LARGEST available size of glazier's points is number   7.__
    A. 3   B. 1   C. 0   D. 000

8. The purpose of priming wood window sash before applying   8.__
putty and glass is to prevent the
    A. putty from absorbing moisture from the wood
    B. putty from staining the wood
    C. wood from absorbing the oils from the putty
    D. natural wood resins from making the putty brittle

9. When hard, dry putty must be removed from a wood window frame in order to put in a new pane of glass, the BEST tool with which to do this job is a
    A. screwdriver   B. putty knife
    C. wide wood chisel   D. pocket knife

9.___

10. Before repainting a wood surface on which the old paint film has developed some wrinkling, the MOST appropriate treatment for the wood surface is a
    A. thorough scraping
    B. light shellacking
    C. wash-down with dilute muriatic acid
    D. rubbing down of the wrinkles with fairly coarse sandpaper

10.___

11. A paint that is characterized by its ability to dry to an especially smooth, hard, glossy or semi-glossy finish is called a(n)
    A. primer   B. sealer   C. glaze   D. enamel

11.___

12. The BEST thinner for varnishes is
    A. gasoline   B. turpentine
    C. kerosene   D. water

12.___

13. To get a good paint job on a new plaster wall, one should make certain that the
    A. wall is thoroughly dry before painting
    B. base coat is much darker than the finishing coat
    C. wall has been roughened enough to make the paint stick
    D. plaster has not completely set

13.___

14. In a three-coat plaster job, the brown coat is applied
    A. *before* the scratch coat has set
    B. *immediately after* the scratch coat
    C. *after* the scratch coat has set and partially dried
    D. *after* the scratch coat has thoroughly dried out

14.___

15. Plaster which has sand as an aggregate, when compared with plaster which has a lightweight aggregate, is
    A. a better sound absorber
    B. a better insulator
    C. less likely to crack under a sharp blow
    D. cheaper

15.___

16. One form of metal lath comes in sheets 27"x96". The number of sheets required to cover 20 square yards without overlap is
    A. 9   B. 10   C. 11   D. 12

16.___

17. When nailing gypsum board lath to studs or furring strips, the nailing should be started _____ of the board.
    A. along the top   B. along the bottom
    C. at the center   D. at one end

17.___

18. A wooden mortar box for slaking lime is lined with sheet   18.__
    iron.
    Of the following, the GREATEST advantage of the lining
    is that
      A. a better grade putty is produced
      B. the box is easier to clean
      C. it makes the box water-tight
      D. it prevents burning of the wood

19. In the city, the building code requires that water used   19.__
    in plastering MUST
      A. be perfectly clear in color
      B. not have any rust in it
      C. be fit for drinking
      D. not be fluoridated

20. In order to prevent thin sheet metal from buckling when   20.__
    riveting it to an angle iron, the BEST procedure is to
      A. start riveting at one end of the sheet and work
         toward the other end
      B. start riveting at both ends of the sheet and work in
         toward the center
      C. install alternate rivets working in one direction,
         and then fill in the remaining rivets working in the
         other direction
      D. start riveting in the center of the joint, working
         out in both directions

KEY (CORRECT ANSWERS)

1. B	11. D
2. B	12. B
3. C	13. A
4. B	14. C
5. B	15. D
6. C	16. B
7. C	17. C
8. C	18. B
9. C	19. C
10. D	20. D

TEST 3

DIRECTIONS: Each question or incomplete statement is followed by
several suggested answers or completions. Select the
one that BEST answers the question or completes the
statement. *PRINT THE LETTER OF THE CORRECT ANSWER IN
THE SPACE AT THE RIGHT.*

1. A drill bit measures .625 inches.   1.___
    The fractional equivalent, in inches, is
        A. 9/16   B. 5/8   C. 11/16   D. 3/4

2. The number of cubic yards of sand required to fill a bin   2.___
    measuring 12 feet by 6 feet by 4 feet is MOST NEARLY
        A. 8   B. 11   C. 48   D. 96

3. Assume that you are assigned to put down floor tiles in a   3.___
    room measuring 8 feet by 10 feet. Individual tiles
    measure 9 inches by 9 inches.
    The TOTAL number of floor tiles required to cover the
    entire floor is MOST NEARLY
        A. 107   B. 121   C. 144   D. 160

4. Lumber is usually sold by the board foot, and a board   4.___
    foot is defined as a board one foot square and one inch
    thick.
    If the price of one board foot of lumber is 90 cents and
    you need 20 feet of lumber 6 inches wide and 1 inch thick,
    the cost of the 20 feet of lumber is
        A. $9.00   B. $12.00   C. $18.00   D. $24.00

5. For a certain plumbing repair job, you need three lengths   5.___
    of pipe, 12¼ inches, 6½ inches, and 8 5/8 inches.
    If you cut these three lengths from the same piece of
    pipe, which is 36 inches long, and each cut consumes 1/8
    inch of pipe, the length of pipe *remaining* after you have
    cut out your three pieces should be _____ inches.
        A. 7¼   B. 7 7/8   C. 8¼   D. 8 7/8

6. When preparing an estimate for a certain repair job, you   6.___
    determine that $250 worth of materials and 220 man-hours
    are required to complete the job.
    If your man-hour cost is $10.50 per hour, the TOTAL cost
    of this repair job is
        A. $2,060   B. $2,310   C. $2,560   D. $2,810

7. Assume that in determining the total cost of a repair job   7.___
    a 15% shop cost is to be added to the costs of material
    and labor.
    For a repair job which cost $200 in materials and $600
    in labor, the shop cost is
        A. $30   B. $60   C. $90   D. $120

8. From experience, you have found that one gallon of primer   8.__
will cover 600 square feet and one gallon of interior
latex flat paint will cover 400 square feet.
If you estimate that a certain repair job has 3,600 square
feet to be painted and that both a coat of primer and a
coat of flat paint are required, the material required for
this job is _____ gallons of primer and _____ gallons of
flat paint.
    A. 6; 6   B. 6; 9   C. 3; 9   D. 9; 6

9. Assume that you have been given a deadline of the close   9.__
of business, Friday, May 10, to complete a certain repair
job. You have estimated that 350 man-hours are required
to complete the job. Your men normally work a 7-hour
day, 5 days per week.
If you start this job on Monday, May 6, the number of men
you MUST assign to this job daily in order to complete it
by the deadline is
    A. 5   B. 10   C. 15   D. 20

10. Assume that from a study of your inventory control card   10.__
for patching plaster, you find that you are issuing 5
one-pound bags per day. Agency policy requires that you
maintain a reserve supply for five days supply on hand
at all times.
If it takes twenty work days to have a requisition for
this item filled, you should submit a requisition for
additional supplies when your balance on hand is
    A. 25   B. 75   C. 100   D. 125

11. After inspecting an abandoned four-story brownstone   11.__
dwelling, the one of the following existing conditions
which should receive FIRST priority for repair work is
    A. broken windows   B. fallen ceilings
    C. missing interior doors   D. stopped-up toilet bowls

12. After conducting inspections of a group of ten two-story   12.__
houses located on the same street, you find that all of
them require some repair work.
In setting up priorities for handling all the repairs
required, the FIRST priority should be given to work
which
    A. eliminates safety hazards
    B. requires the least amount of material
    C. prevents further deterioration of the property
    D. uses excess materials which you have on hand

13. You have assigned a repair crew to begin work on an   13.__
unoccupied sixteen family, four-story walkup apartment
house. The building has no electricity, water, or heat.
In preparing the building for future occupancy, you have
determined that the sequence for accomplishing the
required repairs should be

    A. building security, electricity, water, heat
    B. building security, water, heat, electricity
    C. electricity, building security, heat, water
    D. electricity, heat, water, building security

14. Plans or job specifications to accomplish minor housing   14.___
repair work may be written in a brief or sketchy form
because the
    A. agency rules and regulations cover most repair work
       to be done by a repair shop
    B. costs of complete plans or specifications as custom-
       arily used in the building trades are expensive for
       the size and nature of the work to be done
    C. details of the specification are completed after the
       repair work has been done
    D. unknown factors in making such repairs are unpredic-
       table

15. Of the following, the MOST important reason for having a   15.___
vehicle preventive maintenance and history card is
    A. for use in making vehicle assignments
    B. to check whether the drivers are completing their
       assignments
    C. for use as a control device in scheduling maintenance
    D. as a means for projecting future maintenance expenses

16. In his efforts to maintain standards of performance, a   16.___
shop manager uses a system of close supervision to detect
or catch errors.
An *opposite* method of accomplishing the same objective is
to employ a program which
    A. instills in each employee a pride of workmanship to
       do the job correctly the first time
    B. groups each job according to the importance to the
       overall objectives of the program
    C. makes the control of quality the responsibility of
       an inspector
    D. emphasizes that there is a *one* best way for an
       employee to do a specific job

17. Assume that after taking over a repair shop, a shop   17.___
manager feels that he is taking too much time maintaining
records.
He should
    A. temporarily assign this job to one of his senior
       repair crew chiefs
    B. get together with his supervisor to determine if all
       these records are needed
    C. stop keeping those records which he believes are
       unnecessary
    D. spend a few additional hours each day until his
       records are current

18. In order to apply performance standards to employees engaged in repair shop activities, a shop manager must FIRST
    A. allow workers to decide for themselves the way to do the job
    B. determine what is acceptable as satisfactory work
    C. separate the more difficult tasks from the simpler tasks
    D. stick to an established work schedule

18.___

19. Of the following actions a repair shop manager can take to determine if the vehicles used in his shop are being utilized properly, the one which will give him the LEAST meaningful information is
    A. conducting an analysis of vehicle assignments
    B. reviewing the number of miles traveled by each vehicle with and without loads
    C. recording the unloaded weights of each vehicle
    D. comparing the amount of time vehicles are parked at job sites with the time required to travel to and from job sites

19.___

20. For a shop manager, the MOST important reason that equipment which is used infrequently should be considered for disposal is that
    A. the time required for its maintenance could be better used elsewhere
    B. such equipment may cause higher management to think that your shop is not busy
    C. the men may resent having to work on such equipment
    D. such equipment usually has a higher breakdown rate in operation

20.___

KEY (CORRECT ANSWERS)

1.	B	11.	A
2.	B	12.	A
3.	C	13.	A
4.	A	14.	B
5.	C	15.	C
6.	C	16.	A
7.	D	17.	B
8.	B	18.	B
9.	B	19.	C
10.	D	20.	A

EXAMINATION SECTION

TEST 1

DIRECTIONS: Each question or incomplete statement is followed by several suggested answers or completions. Select the one that BEST answers the question or completes the statement. *PRINT THE LETTER OF THE CORRECT ANSWER IN THE SPACE AT THE RIGHT.*

Questions 1-3.

DIRECTIONS: Questions 1 through 3, inclusive, are to be answered in accordance with the American Standard Graphical Symbols for Pipe Fittings, Valves, and Piping and American Standard Graphical Symbols for Heating, Ventilating and Air Conditioning.

1. The symbol ⊙─┼──── shown on a piping drawing repre-   1.___
    sents a ____ elbow.
    A. turned down   B. reducing
    C. long radius   D. turned up

2. The symbol ──┤▭├── shown on a heating drawing repre-   2.___
    sents a(n)
    A. expansion joint   B. hanger or support
    C. heat exchanger   D. air eliminator

3. The symbol ──┤▷◁├── shown on a piping drawing repre-   3.___
    sents a ____ gate valve.
    A. welded   B. flanged
    C. screwed   D. bell and spigot

4. The MAIN purpose for the inspection of plant equipment,   4.___
    buildings, and facilities is to
    A. determine the quality of maintenance work of all the
       trades
    B. prevent the overstocking of equipment and materials
       used in maintenance work
    C. forecast normal maintenance jobs for existing equipment,
       buildings, and facilities
    D. prevent unscheduled interruptions of operating equip-
       ment and excessive deterioration of buildings and
       facilities

5. Of the following devices, the one that is used to determine   5.___
    the rating, in cubic feet per minute, of a unit ventilator
    is a(n)
    A. psychrometer   B. pyrometer
    C. anemometer   D. manometer

6. A number of 4' x 6' skids loaded with material are to be   6.___
    stored. Assume that the total weight of each loaded skid is
    1200 pounds and that the maximum allowable floor load is
    280 lbs. per sq. ft.

The MAXIMUM number of skids that can be stacked vertically
without exceeding the MAXIMUM allowable floor load is
    A. 4   B. 5   C. 6   D. 7

7. Specifications which contain the term *slump test* would   7.__
    MOST likely refer to
      A. lumber   B. paint   C. concrete   D. water

8. Of the following sizes of copper conductors, the one   8.__
    which has the LEAST current-carrying capacity is ____ AWG.
      A. 000   B. 0   C. 8   D. 12

9. The size of a steel beam is shown on a steel drawing as   9.__
    W 8 x 15.
    In accordance with the latest edition of the Steel Construc-
    tion Manual of the American Institute of Steel Construction,
    the number 8 in W 8 x 15 represents the beam's *approximate*
      A. depth   B. flange thickness
      C. width   D. web thickness

10. For expediting control functions such as work methods,   10.__
    planning, scheduling, and work measurement, EQUIPMENT
    RECORDS must contain specific data.
    Of the following, the data which is NOT usually indicated
    on an EQUIPMENT RECORD card is
      A. machinery and parts specifications numbers
      B. a breakdown history
      C. a preventive maintenance history
      D. salvage value on the open market

11. Refrigeration piping, valves, fittings, and related parts   11.__
    used in the construction and installation of refrigeration
    systems shall conform to the
      A. American Society of Mechanical Engineers Boiler and
         Pressure Vessel Code
      B. American Standards Association Code for Pressure
         Piping
      C. Pipe Fabrication Institute Standards
      D. Underwriters Laboratory Standards

12. The maintenance term *downtime* means MOST NEARLY the   12.__
      A. period of time in which a machine is out of service
      B. routine replacement of parts or materials to a piece
         of equipment
      C. labor required for clean-up of equipment to insure
         its proper operation
      D. maintenance work which is confined to checking,
         adjusting, and lubrication of equipment

13. A supplier quotes a list price of $172.00 less 15 and   13.__
    10 percent for twelve tools.
    The ACTUAL cost for these twelve tools is MOST NEARLY
      A. $146   B. $132   C. $129   D. $112

14. Of the following colors of electrical conductor coverings,   14.__
    the one which indicates a conductor used SOLELY for grounding
    portable or fixed electrical equipment is
      A. blue   B. green   C. red   D. black

15. A *medium duty* type of scaffold is one on which the working   15.___
load on the platform surface must NOT exceed ____ pounds
per square foot.
    A. 50   B. 70   C. 90   D. 110

16. Assume that a mechanic is using a powder-actuated tool   16.___
and the cartridge misfires.
According to recommended safe practices regarding a misfired
cartridge, the FIRST course of action the mechanic should
take is to
    A. place the misfired cartridge carefully into a metal
        container filled with water
    B. carefully reload the tool with the misfired cartridge
        and try it again
    C. immediately bury the misfired cartridge at least two
        feet in the ground
    D. remove the wadding from the misfired cartridge and
        empty the powder into a pail of sand

17. The ratings used in classifying fire resistant building   17.___
construction materials are MOST frequently expressed in
    A. Btu's   B. hours   C. temperatures D. pounds

18. The only legible portion of the nameplate on a piece of   18.___
equipment reads: *208 volts, 3 phase, 10 H.P.*
This data would MOST NEARLY indicate that the piece of
equipment is a(n)
    A. amplifier   B. fixture ballast
    C. motor   D. rectifier

19. Of the following items relating to the maintenance of   19.___
roofs, the one which is of the LEAST value in a preventive
maintenance program for roofs is knowledge of the
    A. roofing specifications   B. application procedures
    C. process of deterioration D. frequency of rainstorms

20. In an oxyacetylene cutting outfit, the color of the hose   20.___
that is connected to the oxygen cylinder is USUALLY
    A. white   B. yellow   C. red   D. green

21. Assume that a welding generator is to be used to weld   21.___
partitions made of 18 gauge steel.
Of the following settings, the BEST one to use would be
a ____ setting of voltage and a ____ setting of amperage.
    A. high; high B. high; low   C. low; high   D. low; low

22. According to the administrative code, when color marking   22.___
is used, potable water lines shall be painted
    A. yellow   B. blue   C. red   D. green

23. A set of mechanical plan drawings is drawn to a scale of   23.___
1/8" = 1 foot.
If a length of pipe measures 15 7/16" on the drawing, the
ACTUAL length of the pipe is ____ feet.
    A. 121.5   B. 122.5   C. 123.5   D. 124.5

24. A portion of a specification states: *Concrete, other*   24.__
than that placed under water, should be compacted and
worked into place by spading or puddling.
The MAIN reason why *spading and puddling* is required is to
    A. insure that all water in the concrete mix is brought
to the surface
    B. eliminate stone pockets and large bubbles of air
    C. provide a means to obtain a spade full of concrete
for test purposes
    D. make allowances for *bleeding and segregation* of the
concrete

25. Assume that the following statement appears in a construc-   25.__
tion contract: *Payment will be made for the number of*
pounds of bar reinforcement incorporated in the work as
shown on the plans.
This type of contract is MOST likely
    A. cost plus   B. lump sum   C. subcontract   D. unit price

26. Partial payments to outside contractors are USUALLY based   26.__
on the
    A. breakdown estimate submitted after the contract was
signed
    B. actual cost of labor and material plus overhead and
profit
    C. estimate of work completed which is generally submitted
periodically
    D. estimate of material delivered to the job

27. Building contracts usually require that estimates for   27.__
changes made in the field be submitted for approval before
the work can start.
The MAIN reason for this requirement is to
    A. make sure that the contractor understands the change
    B. discourage such changes
    C. keep the contractor honest
    D. enable the department to control its expenses

28. An *addendum* to contract specifications means MOST NEARLY   28.__
    A. a substantial completion payment to the contractor
for work almost completed
    B. final acceptance of the work by authorities of all
contract work still to be done
    C. additional contract provisions issued in writing by
authorities prior to receipt of bids
    D. work other than that required by the contract at the
time of its execution

29. Of the following terms, the one which is usually NOT used   29.__
to describe the types of payments to outside contractors
for work done is the ____ payment.
    A. partial payment   B. substantial completion
    C. final   D. surety

30. Of the following metals, the one which is a ferrous metal is   30.____
      A. cast iron   B. brass   C. bronze   D. babbit

31. Assume that you have assigned six mechanics to do a job   31.____
    that must be finished in four days. At the end of three
    days, your men have completed only two-thirds of the job.
    In order to complete the job on time and because the job
    is such that it cannot be speeded up, you should assign a
    MINIMUM of ____ extra men.
      A. 3   B. 4   C. 5   D. 6

32. Of the following traps, the one which is NORMALLY used to   32.____
    retain steam in a heating unit or piping is the ____ trap.
      A. P   B. running   C. float   D. bell

33. Of the following materials, the one which is a convenient   33.____
    and powerful adhesive for cementing tears in canvas jackets
    that are wrapped around warm pipe insulation is
      A. cylinder oil   B. wheat paste
      C. water glass   D. latex paint

34. Pipe chases should be provided with an access door   34.____
    PRIMARILY to provide means to
      A. replace piping lines
      B. either inspect or manipulate valves
      C. prevent condensate from forming on the pipes
      D. check the chase for possible structural defects

35. Electric power is measured in   35.____
      A. volts   B. amperes   C. watts   D. ohms

____

KEY (CORRECT ANSWERS)

1. D	11. B	21. B	31. A
2. A	12. A	22. D	32. C
3. B	13. B	23. C	33. C
4. D	14. B	24. B	34. B
5. C	15. A	25. D	35. C
6. B	16. A	26. C	
7. C	17. B	27. D	
8. D	18. C	28. C	
9. A	19. D	29. D	
10. D	20. D	30. A	

TEST 2

DIRECTIONS: Each question or incomplete statement is followed by several suggested answers or completions. Select the one that BEST answers the question or completes the statement. *PRINT THE LETTER OF THE CORRECT ANSWER IN THE SPACE AT THE RIGHT.*

1. The HIGHEST quality tools should
   A. always be bought
   B. never be bought
   C. be bought when they offer an overall advantage
   D. be bought only for foreman

   1.___

2. Master keys should have no markings that will identify them as such.
   This statement is
   A. *false*; it would be impossible to keep records about them without such markings
   B. *true*; markings are subject to alteration and vandalization
   C. *false*; without such markings, they would be too lightly regarded by those to whom issued
   D. *true*; markings would only highlight their value to a potential wrongdoer

   2.___

3. For a foreman to usually delay for a few weeks handling grievances his men make is a
   A. *poor* practice; it can affect the morale of the men
   B. *good* practice; it will discourage grievances
   C. *poor* practice; the causes of grievances usually disappear if action is delayed
   D. *good* practice; most employee grievances are not justified

   3.___

4. Whenever an important change in procedure is contemplated, some foremen make a point of discussing the matter with their subordinates in order to get their viewpoint on the proposed change.
   In general, this practice is advisable MAINLY for the reason that
   A. subordinates can often see the effects of procedural changes more clearly than foremen
   B. the foreman has an opportunity to explain the advantages of the new procedure
   C. future changes will be welcomed if subordinates are kept informed
   D. participation in work planning helps to build a spirit of cooperation among employees

   4.___

5. An estimate of employee morale could LEAST effectively be appraised by
   A. checking accident and absenteeism records
   B. determining the attitudes of employees toward their job

   5.___

      C. examining the number of requests for emergency leaves
         of absence
      D. reviewing the number and nature of employee suggestions

6. Assume that you are a foreman and that a visitor at the   6.___
   job site asks you what your crew is doing.
   You should
   - A. respectfully decline to answer since all questions
     must be answered by the proper authority
   - B. answer as concisely as possible but discourage undue
     conversation
   - C. refer the man to your superiors
   - D. give the person complete details of the job

7. Cooperation can BEST be obtained from the general public by   7.___
   - A. siding with them whenever they have a complaint
   - B. sticking carefully to your work and ignoring every-
     thing else
   - C. explaining the department's objectives and why the
     public must occasionally be temporarily inconvenienced
   - D. listening politely to their complaints and telling them
     that the complaints will be forwarded to the main office

8. While you are working for the city, a man says to you that   8.___
   one of the rules of your job doesn't make sense and he gets
   mad.
   You should say to him
   - A. Leave me alone so I can get my work done
   - B. Everyone must follow the rules
   - C. Let me tell you the reason for the rule
   - D. I'm only doing my job so don't get mad at me

9. One approach to preparing written reports to superiors is   9.___
   to present first the conclusions and recommendations and
   then the data on which the conclusions and recommendations
   are based.
   The use of this approach is BEST justified when the
   - A. data completely support the conclusions and recommenda-
     tions
   - B. superiors lack the specific training and experience
     required to understand and interpret the data
   - C. data contain more information than is required for
     making the conclusions and recommendations
   - D. superiors are more interested in the conclusions and
     recommendations than in the data

10. The MOST important reason why separate paragraphs might be   10.___
    used in writing a report is that this
    - A. makes it easier to understand the report
    - B. permits the report to be condensed
    - C. gives a better appearance to the report
    - D. prevents accidental elimination of important facts

11. On a drawing, the following standard cross-section represents MOST NEARLY 11.__

    A. sand   B. concrete   C. earth   D. rock

12. On a drawing, the following standard cross-section represents MOST NEARLY 12.__

    A. malleable iron   B. steel
    C. bronze   D. lead

13. On a piping plan drawing, the symbol represents a 90° ____ elbow. 13.__
    A. flanged   B. screwed
    C. bell and spigot   D. welded

14. On a drawing, the symbol represents 14.__

    A. stone   B. steel   C. glass   D. wood

15. On a heating piping drawing, the symbol represents ____ piping. 15.__
    A. high-pressure steam   B. medium-pressure steam
    C. low-pressure   D. hot water supply

16. Of the following devices, the one that is LEAST frequently used to attach a piece of equipment to concrete or masonry walls is a(n) 16.__
    A. carriage bolt   B. through bolt
    C. lag screw   D. expansion bolt

17. A vapor barrier is usually installed in conjunction with 17.__
    A. drainage piping   B. roof flashing
    C. building insulation   D. wood sheathing

Questions 18-20.

DIRECTIONS: Questions 18 through 20 are to be answered in accordance with the following table.

	Man Days Borough 1 Oct. Nov.		Man Days Borough 2 Oct. Nov.		Man Days Borough 3 Oct. Nov.		Man Days Borough 4 Oct. Nov.	
Carpenter	70	100	35	180	145	205	120	85
Plumber	95	135	195	100	70	130	135	80
House Painter	90	90	120	80	85	85	95	195
Electrician	120	110	135	155	120	95	70	205
Blacksmith	125	145	60	180	205	145	80	125

18. In accordance with the above table, if the average daily pay of the five trades listed above is $47.50, the approximate labor cost of work done by the five trades during the month of October for Borough 1 is MOST NEARLY 18.__
    A. $22,800   B. $23,450   C. $23,750   D. $26,125

19. In accordance with the above table, the Borough which MOST   19.___
    NEARLY made up 22.4% of the total plumbing work force for
    the month of November is Borough
    A. 1   B. 2   C. 3   D. 4

20. In accordance with the above table, the average man days   20.___
    per month per Borough spent on electrical work for all
    Boroughs combined is MOST NEARLY
    A. 120   B. 126   C. 130   D. 136

21. Of the following percentages of carbon, the one that   21.___
    would indicate a medium carbon steel is
    A. 0.2%   B. 0.4%   C. 0.8%   D. 1.2%

22. A *screw pitch gage* measures only the   22.___
    A. looseness of threads
    B. tightness of threads
    C. number of threads per inch
    D. gage number

23. Assume that you are to make an inspection of a building   23.___
    to determine the need for painting.
    Of the following tools, the one which is LEAST needed to
    aid you in your inspection is a
    A. sharp penknife   B. putty knife
    C. lightweight tack hammer   D. six-foot rule

24. A *slump test* for concrete is used MAINLY to measure the   24.___
    concrete's
    A. strength   B. consistency   C. flexibility   D. porosity

25. Specifications which contain the term *kiln dried* would   25.___
    MOST likely refer to
    A. asphalt shingles   B. brick veneer
    C. paint lacquer   D. lumber

26. In accordance with established jurisdictional work proce-   26.___
    dures among the trades, the person you would assign to
    replace a malfunctioning fire sprinkler head would be a
    A. plumber   B. laborer   C. housesmith   D. steamfitter

27. Of the following types of union shops, the one which is   27.___
    illegal under the Taft-Hartley Law is the ____ shop.
    A. closed   B. open
    C. union   D. union representative

28. Of the following types of contracts, the one that in city   28.___
    work would MOST likely be limited to emergency work *only* is
    A. lump-sum
    B. unit-price
    C. cost-plus
    D. partial cost-plus and lump-sum

29. Of the following qualifications of outside work contractors,   29.___
    the one which is the LEAST important requirement for deter-
    mining eligible contractors is
    A. availability   B. size of work force
    C. experience   D. location of business

30. Of the following piping materials, the one that combines the physical strength of mild steel with the corrosion resistance of gray iron is
    A. grade A steel   B. grey cast iron
    C. welded wrought iron   D. ductile iron
30.__

31. Assume that a can of red lead paint needs to be thinned slightly.
Of the following, the one that should be used is
    A. turpentine   B. lacquer thinner
    C. water   D. alcohol
31.__

32. Assume that a trench is 42" wide, 5' deep, and 100' long. If the unit price of excavating the trench is $35 per cubic yard, the cost of excavating the trench is MOST NEARLY
    A. $2,275   B. $5,110   C. $7,000   D. $21,000
32.__

33. Of the following uses, the one for which a bituminous compound would usually be used is to
    A. prevent corrosion of burled steel tanks
    B. increase the strength of concrete
    C. caulk water pipes
    D. paint inside wood columns
33.__

34. An electrical drawing is drawn to a scale of $\frac{1}{4}$" = 1'. If a length of conduit on the drawing measures 7 3/8", the actual length of the conduit, in feet, is MOST NEARLY
    A. 7.5'   B. 15.5'   C. 22.5'   D. 29.5'
34.__

35. Of the following steam heating systems, the one that operates under both vacuum and low pressure conditions, without using a vacuum pump, is generally known as a ____ system.
    A. one pipe low pressure   B. vacuum
    C. vapor   D. high pressure
35.__

36. Of the following valve trim symbols, the one which designates a valve trim made of monel material is
    A. 8-18   B. NI-CU   C. SM   D. MI
36.__

37. A replacement part for a piece of equipment is to be made of S.A.E. 4047 steel.
This material is MOST likely a ____ steel.
    A. wrought   B. nickel
    C. chrome-vanadium   D. molybdenum
37.__

38. A metallic underground water piping system is to be used as a means of grounding.
Of the following statements concerning use of this system, the one that is MOST NEARLY CORRECT is that this use is
    A. not permitted
    B. permitted where available
    C. absolutely required
    D. permitted only in certain cases
38.__

39. For pipe sizes up to 8", schedule 40 pipe is identical to
   ____ pipe.
       A. standard   B. extra strong
       C. double extra strong   D. type M copper

39.___

40. Assume that a shop is undergoing a general housecleaning,
    and all excess unused materials have been removed.
    Clean-up work, as pertains to painting in this case,
    means MOST NEARLY
       A. a thorough two-coat paint job
       B. only that surface which was marred to be painted
       C. a one-coat job to *freshen things up*
       D. only that iron work is to be painted

40.___

41. The *United States Standard Gage* is used to measure sheet
    metal thicknesses of
       A. iron and steel   B. aluminum
       C. copper   D. tin

41.___

42. Headers and stretchers are used in the construction of
       A. floors   B. walls   C. ceilings   D. roofs

42.___

Questions 43-44.

DIRECTIONS: Questions 43 and 44, inclusive, are to be answered in
               accordance with the following paragraph.

*For cast iron pipe lines, the middle ring or sleeve shall have
beveled ends and shall be high quality cast iron. The middle ring
shall have a minimum wall thickness of 3/8" for pipe up to 8", 7/16"
for pipe 10" to 30", and ½" for pipe over 30", nominal diameter.
Minimum length of middle ring shall be 5" for pipe up to 10", 6" for
pipe 10" to 30", and 10" for pipe 30" nominal diameter and larger.
The middle ring shall not have a center pipe stop, unless otherwise
specified.*

43. As used in the above paragraph, the word *beveled* means
    MOST NEARLY
       A. straight   B. slanted   C. curved   D. rounded

43.___

44. In accordance with the above paragraph, the middle ring of
    a 24" nominal diameter pipe would have a minimum wall thick-
    ness and length of ____ thick and ____ long.
       A. 3/8"; 5"   B. 3/8"; 6"   C. 7/16"; 6"   D. 1/2"; 6"

44.___

45. A work order is NOT usually issued for which one of the
    following jobs:
       A. Repairing wood door frames
       B. Taking daily inventory
       C. Installing electric switches in maintenance shop
       D. Repairing a number of valves in boiler room

45.___

46. Of the following statements, the one which usually does
    NOT pertain to preventative maintenance programs is
       A. periodic inspection of facilities
       B. lubrication of equipment
       C. minor repair of equipment
       D. complete replacement of deteriorated equipment

46.___

Questions 47-50.

DIRECTIONS: Questions 47 through 50, inclusive, are based on the
sketch of metal sheet shown below. (Sketch not to scale.)

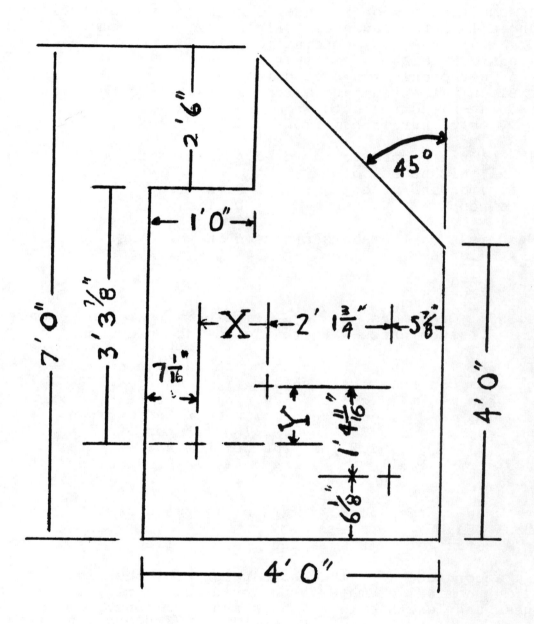

47. From the above sketch, the distance marked X 47.___
    is MOST NEARLY
    A. 5¼"   B. 6 5/16"   C. 7 1/8"   D. 9 5/16"

48. From the above sketch, the distance marked Y 48.___
    is MOST NEARLY
    A. 5 11/16"   B. 6 3/16"   C. 7 5/16"   D. 8 11/16"

49. In reference to the above sketch, if each piece is made   49.___
    from a rectangular piece of metal measuring 4' x 7', the
    percent of waste material is MOST NEARLY
        A. 10%   B. 15%   C. 25%   D. 30%

50. In reference to the above sketch, if the metal is $\frac{1}{4}$" thick   50.___
    and weighs 144 pounds per cubic foot, the net weight of
    one piece would be MOST NEARLY ____ pounds.
        A. 51   B. 63   C. 75   D. 749

KEY (CORRECT ANSWERS)

1. C	11. A	21. B	31. A	41. A
2. D	12. C	22. C	32. A	42. B
3. A	13. A	23. D	33. A	43. B
4. D	14. D	24. B	34. D	44. C
5. C	15. B	25. D	35. C	45. B
6. B	16. A	26. D	36. B	46. D
7. C	17. C	27. A	37. D	47. D
8. C	18. C	28. C	38. B	48. D
9. D	19. B	29. D	39. A	49. C
10. A	20. B	30. D	40. C	50. B

EXAMINATION SECTION
TEST 1

DIRECTIONS: Each question or incomplete statement is followed by several suggested answers or completions. Select the one that BEST answers the question or completes the statement. *PRINT THE LETTER OF THE CORRECT ANSWER IN THE SPACE AT THE RIGHT.*

1. A maintenance man complains to you that he is getting all the boring jobs to do. You check and find that his complaint has no basis in fact.
The one of the following which is the MOST likely reason why the maintenance man made such a claim is that he
   A. wants to get even with the supervisor
   B. lives in a world of fantasy
   C. believes the injustice to be real
   D. is jealous of other workers

1.____

2. When on preliminary review of a mechanic's written grievance you feel the grievance to be unfounded, the FIRST step you should take is to
   A. show the mechanic where he is wrong
   B. check carefully to find out why the mechanic thinks that way
   C. try to humor the mechanic out of it
   D. tell the mechanic to stop complaining

2.____

3. Assume that you decide to hold a private meeting with one of your mechanics who has a drinking problem that is affecting his work.
At the meeting, the BEST way for you to handle this situation is to
   A. tell the mechanic off and then listen to what he has to say
   B. criticize the mechanic's behavior to get him to *open up* in order to help him correct his problem quickly
   C. try to get the mechanic to recognize his problem and find ways to solve it
   D. limit the discussion to matters concerning only the problem and look for immediate results

3.____

4. The one of the following which is a generally accepted guide in criticizing a subordinate EFFECTIVELY is to
   A. criticize the improper act, not the individual
   B. put the listener on the defensive
   C. make the criticism general instead of specific
   D. correct the personality, not the situation

4.____

5. The one of the following disciplinary methods by which you are MOST likely to be successful in getting a problem employee to improve his behavior is when you

5.____

A. discipline the employee in front of others
B. consider the matter to be ended after the disciplining
C. give the exact same discipline no matter how serious the wrongdoing
D. make an example of the employee

6. Of the following statements, the one that is MOST applicable to a disciplinary situation is that discipline should be
    A. used after a cooling-off period
    B. identical for all employees
    C. consistent with the violation
    D. based on personal feelings

    6.___

7. The one of the following approaches that is MOST important for you to take in evaluating a mechanic in order to increase his work productivity is to
    A. first have him evaluate his own performance
    B. meet with him to discuss how he is doing and what is expected on the job
    C. send him a copy of your evaluation of his work performance and give him the opportunity to submit written comments
    D. express in writing your appreciation of his work

    7.___

8. Assume that you say to one of the mechanics, *Jim, that job you turned out today was top-notch. I didn't think you could do so well with the kind of material you had to work with.*
This statement BEST describes an example of your
    A. recognition of the man's work
    B. disrespect for the man's feelings
    C. personal favoritism of the man
    D. constructive criticism of the man's work

    8.___

9. In general, the OUTSTANDING characteristic of employees over 50 years of age is their
    A. resistance   B. endurance
    C. wisdom   D. job stability

    9.___

10. You should be interested in the morale of your men because morale is MOST often associated with
    A. mechanization   B. automation
    C. production   D. seniority regulations

    10.___

11. Assume that the maintenance work order system is about to be changed. Your workers would MOST likely show the LEAST resistance to this change if you
    A. downgrade the old maintenance work order system
    B. tell your workers how the change will benefit them
    C. post the notice of the change on the bulletin board
    D. tell the workers how the change will benefit management

    11.___

12. Of the following, the BEST way to motivate a newly   12.____
    appointed mechanic is to
        A. explain the meaning of each assignment
        B. make the work more physically demanding
        C. test the mechanic's ability
        D. use as much authority as possible

13. The one of the following which is the LEAST important   13.____
    reason for giving employees information concerning
    policy changes which will affect them is that employees
    should know
        A. why the change is being made
        B. who will be affected by the change
        C. when the change will go into effect
        D. how much savings will be made by the change

14. A foreman who knows how to handle his men will MOST   14.____
    likely get them to produce more by treating them
        A. alike   B. as individuals
        C. on a casual basis   D. as a group

15. Of the following items, the one that a supervisor has the   15.____
    MOST right to expect from his employees is
        A. liking the job
        B. a fair day's work
        C. equal skill of all mechanics
        D. perfection

16. The one of the following which is the BEST practice for   16.____
    you to follow in handling a dispute between the workers
    is to
        A. side with one of the workers so as to end the dispute
           quickly
        B. pay no attention to the dispute and let the workers
           settle it themselves
        C. listen to each worker's story of the dispute and
           then decide how to settle it
        D. discuss the dispute with other workers and then
           decide how to settle it

17. You are likely to run into an employee morale problem   17.____
    when assigning a dirty job that comes up often.
    Of the following, the BEST method of assigning this work
    is to
        A. rotate this assignment
        B. assign it to the fastest worker
        C. assign it by seniority
        D. assign it to the least skilled worker

18. Of the following, the one that is generally regarded as   18.____
    the BEST aid to high work productivity of subordinates
    is a supervisor's skill in
        A. record keeping
        B. technical work
        C. setting up rules and regulations
        D. human relations

19. The BEST way to help a mechanic who comes to you for
advice on a personal problem is to
    A. listen to the worker's problem without passing judg-
       ment
    B. tell the worker to forget about the problem and to
       stop letting it interfere with his work
    C. talk about your own personal problems to the worker
    D. mind your own business and leave the worker alone

19.____

20. You are in charge of the maintenance shop and have learned
that within the next two weeks the maintenance shop will
be moved to a new location on the plant grounds, but you
have not learned why this move is taking place. Assume
that you have decided not to keep this information from
your mechanics until the reason is known but to inform
them of this matter now.
Of the following, which one is the BEST argument that can
be made regarding your decision?
    A. *Acceptable*; because although the reason is not now
       known, the mechanics will eventually find out about
       the move
    B. *Unacceptable*; because the mechanics do not know at
       this time the reason for the move and this will cause
       anxiety on their part
    C. *Acceptable*; because the mechanics will be affected by
       the move and they should be told what is happening
    D. *Unacceptable*; because the mechanics' advance know-
       ledge of the move will tend to slow down their work
       output

20.____

21. Of the following, the FIRST action for a foreman to take
in making a decision is to
    A. get all the facts
    B. develop alternate solutions
    C. get opinions of others
    D. know the results in advance

21.____

22. Assume that you have just been promoted to foreman.
Of the following, the BEST practice to follow regarding
your previous experience at the mechanic's level is to
    A. continue to fraternize with your old friends
    B. use this experience to better understand those who
       now work for you
    C. use your old connections to keep top management
       informed of mechanics' views
    D. forget the mechanics' points of view

22.____

23. You have decided to hold regular group discussions with
your subordinates on various aspects of their duties.
Of the following methods you might use to begin such a
program, the one which is likely to be MOST productive
is to
    A. express your own ideas and persuade the group to
       accept them

23.____

B. save time and cover more ground by asking questions calling for yes or no answers
C. propose to the group a general plan of action rather than specific ideas carefully worked out
D. provide an informal atmosphere for the exchange of ideas

24. The principle of learning by which a foreman might get the BEST results in training his subordinates is:
    A. Letting the learner discover and correct his own mistakes
    B. Teaching the most technical part of the work first
    C. Teaching all parts of the work during the first training session
    D. Getting the learner to use as many of his five senses as possible

24.___

25. A new mechanic is to be trained to do an involved operation containing several steps of varying difficulty. This mechanic will MOST likely learn the operation more quickly if he is taught
    A. each step in its proper order
    B. the hardest steps first
    C. the easiest steps first
    D. first the steps that do not require tools.

25.___

———

KEY (CORRECT ANSWERS)

1. C		11. B	
2. B		12. A	
3. C		13. D	
4. A		14. B	
5. B		15. B	
6. C		16. C	
7. B		17. A	
8. A		18. D	
9. D		19. A	
10. C		20. C	

21. A
22. B
23. D
24. D
25. C

———

TEST 2

DIRECTIONS: Each question or incomplete statement is followed by several suggested answers or completions. Select the one that BEST answers the question or completes the statement. *PRINT THE LETTER OF THE CORRECT ANSWER IN THE SPACE AT THE RIGHT.*

1. The one of the following job situations in which it is better to give a written order than an oral order is when
   A. the job involves many details
   B. you can check the job's progress easily
   C. the job is repetitive in nature
   D. there is an emergency

   1.____

2. Which one of the following serves as the BEST guideline for you to follow for effective written reports? Keep sentences
   A. short and limit sentences to one thought
   B. short and use as many thoughts as possible
   C. long and limit sentences to one thought
   D. long and use as many thoughts as possible

   2.____

3. Of the following, the BEST reason why a foreman generally should not do the work of an individual mechanic is that
   A. the shop's production figures will not be accurate
   B. a foreman is paid to supervise
   C. the foreman must maintain his authority
   D. the employee may become self-conscious

   3.____

4. One method by which a foreman might prepare written reports to management is to begin with the conclusions, results, or summary and to follow this with the supporting data. The BEST reason why management may prefer this form of report is because
   A. management lacks the specific training to understand the data
   B. the data completely supports the conclusions
   C. time is saved by getting to the conclusions of the report first
   D. the data contains all the information that is required for making the conclusions

   4.____

5. Forms used for time records and work orders are important to the work of a foreman PRIMARILY because they give him
   A. the knowledge of and familiarity with work operations
   B. the means of control of personnel, material, or job costs
   C. the means for communicating with other workers
   D. a useful method for making filing procedures easier

   5.____

6. The one of the following which is the MOST important   6.___
   factor in determining the number of employees you can
   effectively supervise is the
       A. type of work to be performed
       B. priority of the work to be performed
       C. salary level of the workers
       D. ratio of permanent employees to temporary employees

7. Of the following, you will be MOST productive in carrying   7.___
   out your supervisory responsibilities if you
       A. are capable of doing the same work as your mechanics
       B. meet with your mechanics frequently
       C. are very friendly with your mechanics
       D. get work done through your mechanics

8. You have been asked to prepare the annual budget for your   8.___
   maintenance shop.
   The one of the following which is the FIRST step you
   should take in preparing this budget is to determine the
       A. amount of maintenance work which is scheduled for the
          shop
       B. time it takes for a specific unit of work to be
          completed
       C. current workload of each employee in the shop
       D. policies and procedures of the shop's operations

9. When determining the amount of work you expect a group of   9.___
   mechanics to perform in a given time, the BEST procedure
   for you to follow should be to
       A. aim for a higher level of production than that of
          the most productive worker
       B. stay at the present production level
       C. set general instead of specific goals
       D. let workers participate in the determination whenever
          possible

10. You have been asked to set next year's performance goals   10.___
    concerning the ratio of jobs completed on schedule to
    total jobs worked. A review of last year's record shows
    that the workers completed their jobs on schedule 85% of
    the time, with the best ones showing an on-time ratio of
    92% and the poorest ones showing an on-time ratio of 65%.
    Using these facts in line with generally accepted goal-
    setting practices, you should set a performance ratio
    for the next year on the basis of _____ average with a
        _____ minimum acceptable for any employee.
        A. 85%; 65%   B. 85%; 70%   C. 90%; 65%   D. 90%; 70%

11. It is important for you to be able to identify the   11.___
    critical parts of a large project such as the remodeling
    of your maintenance shop.
    The one of the following which is the BEST reason why
    this is important is that it may
        A. help you to set up good communications between you
           and your workers

B. give you a better understanding of the purpose of the project
C. give you control over the time and cost involved in the project
D. help you to determine who are your most productive workers

12. When doing work planning for your shop, the factor that you should normally consider LAST among the following is knowing your

    A. major objectives   B. record keeping system
    C. minor objectives   D. priorities

12.____

13. You have the responsibility for ordering all materials for your maintenance shop. A listing of materials needed for the operations of your shop is long overdue. You realize that you are unable to find time to take care of the inventory personally because of a high priority project you have been working on which has been taking all of your time. You do not know when you will be finished with the project.
The BEST of the following courses of action to take in handling this inventory matter is to

    A. request that you be taken off the project immediately so that you may take care of the inventory
    B. complete your high priority project and then do the inventory yourself
    C. volunteer to work overtime so that you may complete the inventory while continuing with the project
    D. assign the inventory work to a competent subordinate

13.____

14. You have the authority and responsibility for seeing that proper records are kept in your shop. Assume that you decide to delegate to a records clerk the responsibility for collecting the time sheets and the authority to make changes on the time sheets to correct the information when necessary.
Of the following, which one is the BEST argument that can be made regarding your decision?

    A. *Unacceptable*; because you can delegate only your responsibility but none of your authority to the records clerk
    B. *Acceptable*; because you can delegate some of your authority and some of your responsibility to the records clerk
    C. *Unacceptable*; because you can delegate only your authority but none of your responsibility to the records clerk
    D. *Acceptable*; because you can delegate all your responsibility and all your authority to the records clerk

14.____

15. You will LEAST likely be able to do an effective job of   15.___
    controlling operating costs if you
        A. eliminate idle time   B. reduce absenteeism
        C. raise your budget   D. combine work operations

16. Of the following actions, the one which is LEAST likely to   16.___
    help in carrying out your responsibilities of looking
    after the interests of your workers is to
        A. crack down on your workers when necessary
        B. let your workers know that you support company policy
        C. prevent the transfers of your workers
        D. back up your workers in a controversy

17. The term *accountability*, as used in management of super-   17.___
    vision, means MOST NEARLY
        A. responsibility for results
        B. record keeping
        C. bookkeeping systems
        D. inventory control

18. Assume that you have been unable to convince an employee   18.___
    of the seriousness of his poor attendance record by talk-
    ing to him.
    The one of the following which is the BEST course of
    action for you to take is to
        A. keep talking to the employee
        B. recommend that a written warning be given
        C. consider transferring the employee to another work
           location
        D. recommend that the employee be fired

19. When delegating work to a subordinate foreman, you should   19.___
    NOT
        A. delegate the right to make any decisions
        B. be interested in the results of the work, but in
           the method of doing the work
        C. delegate any work that you can do better than your
           subordinate
        D. give up your final responsibility for the work

20. Of the following statements, the BEST reason why proper   20.___
    scheduling of maintenance work is important is that it
        A. eliminates the need for individual job work orders
        B. classifies job skills in accordance with performance
        C. minimizes lost time in performing any maintenance
           job
        D. determines needed repairs in various locations

21. Of the following factors, the one which is of LEAST im-   21.___
    portance in determining the number of subordinates that
    an individual should be assigned to supervise is the
        A. nature of the work being supervised
        B. qualifications of the individual as a supervisor
        C. capabilities of the subordinates
        D. lines of promotion for the subordinates

22. Suppose that a large number of semi-literate residents
    of this city have been requesting the assistance of your
    department. You are asked to prepare a form which these
    applicants will be required to fill out before their
    requests will be considered.
    In view of these facts, the one of the following factors
    to which you should give the GREATEST amount of consi-
    deration in preparing this form is the
    A. size of the form
    B. sequence of the information asked for on the form
    C. level of difficulty of the language used in the form
    D. number of times which the form will have to be
       reviewed

23. A budget is a plan whereby a goal is set for future
    operations. It affords a medium for comparing actual
    expenditures with planned expenditures.
    The one of the following which is the MOST accurate
    statement on the basis of this statement is that
    A. the budget serves as an accurate measure of past as
       well as future expenditures
    B. the budget presents an estimate of expenditures to
       be made in the future
    C. budget estimates should be based upon past budget
       requirements
    D. planned expenditures usually fall short of actual
       expenditures

24. A foreman who is familiar with modern management princi-
    ples should know that the one of the following require-
    ments of an administrator which is LEAST important is
    his ability to
    A. coordinate work
    B. plan, organize, and direct the work under his control
    C. cooperate with others
    D. perform the duties of the employees under his juris-
       diction

25. The one of the following which should be considered the
    LEAST important objective of the service rating system
    is to
    A. rate the employees on the basis of their potential
       abilities
    B. establish a basis for assigning employees to special
       types of work
    C. provide a means of recognizing superior work per-
       formance
    D. reveal the need for training as well as the effec-
       tiveness of a training program

KEY (CORRECT ANSWERS)

1. A	11. C
2. A	12. B
3. B	13. D
4. C	14. B
5. B	15. C
6. A	16. C
7. D	17. A
8. A	18. B
9. D	19. D
10. D	20. C

21. D
22. C
23. B
24. D
25. A

EXAMINATION SECTION
TEST 1

DIRECTIONS: Each question or incomplete statement is followed by several suggested answers or completions. Select the one that BEST answers the question or completes the statement. *PRINT THE LETTER OF THE CORRECT ANSWER IN THE SPACE AT THE RIGHT.*

1. The specification states: *The value of each change order shall be computed separately by cost of labor and materials, plus equipment allowance, plus overhead and profit.*
   The MOST probable value of overhead and profit is _____% of the cost of labor and materials plus equipment allowance.
   A. 5   B. 15   C. 34   D. 55   1.___

2. In the specifications is an item: *Equipment Allowance: Shall include rental of necessary equipment plus 9% of this rental.*
   According to the above specification, if a piece of equipment rents for $35 per day, Equipment Allowance for this equipment rented for 11 days is MOST NEARLY
   A. $484.00   B. $378.42   C. $385.00   D. $419.65   2.___

3. A supplier quotes a list price of $172.00 less 15 and 10 percent for twelve tools.
   The ACTUAL cost for these twelve tools is MOST NEARLY
   A. $146   B. $132   C. $129   D. $112   3.___

4. Which one of the following is the PRIMARY object in drawing up a set of specifications for materials to be purchased?   4.___
   A. Control of quality
   B. Outline of intended use
   C. Establishment of standard sizes
   D. Location and method of inspection

5. In order to avoid disputes over payments for extra work in a contract for construction, the BEST procedure to follow would be to   5.___
   A. have contractor submit work progress reports daily
   B. insert a special clause in the contract specifications
   C. have a representative on the job at all times to verify conditions
   D. allocate a certain percentage of the cost of the job to cover such expenses

6. You wish to order sponges in the most economical manner. Keeping in mind that large sponges can be cut up into many smaller sizes, the one of the following that has the LEAST cost per cubic inch of sponge is _____ sponges @ _____.   6.___
   A. 2" x 4" x 6"; $.24   B. 4" x 8" x 12"; $1.44
   C. 4" x 6" x 36"; $4.80   D. 6" x 8" x 32"; $9.60

7. The cost of a certain job is broken down as follows: **7.___**

Materials	$375
Rental of equipment	120
Labor	315

   The percentage of the total cost of the job that can be charged to materials is MOST NEARLY _____ %.
   A. 40   B. 42   C. 44   D. 46

8. Partial payments to outside contractors are USUALLY based on the **8.___**
   A. breakdown estimate submitted after the contract was signed
   B. actual cost of labor and material plus overhead and profit
   C. estimate of work completed which is generally submitted periodically
   D. estimate of material delivered to the job

9. Building contracts usually require that estimates for changes made in the field be submitted for approval before the work can start. **9.___**
   The MAIN reason for this requirement is to
   A. make sure that the contractor understands the change
   B. discourage such changes
   C. keep the contractor honest
   D. enable the department to control its expenses

10. If the cost of a broom went up from $4.00 to $6.00, the percent INCREASE in the original cost is **10.___**
    A. 20   B. 25   C. 33 1/3   D. 50

11. The AVERAGE of the numbers 3, 5, 7, 8, 12 is **11.___**
    A. 5   B. 6   C. 7   D. 8

12. The cost of 100 bags of cotton cleaning cloths, 89 pounds per bag, at 7 cents per pound is **12.___**
    A. $549.35   B. $623.00   C. $700.00   D. $890.00

13. If 5½ bags of sweeping compound cost $55,00, then 6½ bags would cost **13.___**
    A. $60.00   B. $62.50   C. $65.00   D. $67.00

14. The cost of cleaning supplies in a project averaged $330.00 a month during the first 8 months of the year. How much can be spent each month for the last four months if the total amount that can be spent for cleaning supplies for the year is $3,880? **14.___**
    A. $124   B. $220   C. $310   D. $330

15. The cost of rawl plugs is $2.75 per gross. The cost of 2,448 rawl plugs is **15.___**
    A. $46.75   B. $47.25   C. $47.75   D. $48.25

16. A caretaker received $70.00 for having worked from Monday   16.___
    through Friday, 9 A.M. to 5 P.M. with one hour a day for
    lunch.
    The number of hours the caretaker would have to work to
    earn $12.00 is
    A. 10   B. 6
    C. 70 divided by 12   D. 70 minus 12

17. Assume that an employee is paid at the rate of $5.43 per   17.___
    hour with time and a half for overtime past 40 hours in
    a week.
    If he works 43 hours in a week, his gross weekly pay is
    A. $217.20   B. $219.20   C. $229.59   D. $241.64

18. Kerosene costs 36 cents a quart.   18.___
    At that rate, two gallons would cost
    A. $1.44   B. $2.16   C. $2.88   D. $3.60

Questions 19-21.

DIRECTIONS: Questions 19 through 21 are to be answered on the
            basis of the following table.

	Man Days Borough 1		Man Days Borough 2		Man Days Borough 3		Man Days Borough 4	
	Oct.	Nov.	Oct.	Nov.	Oct.	Nov.	Oct.	Nov.
Carpenter	70	100	35	180	145	205	120	85
Plumber	95	135	195	100	70	130	135	80
House Painter	90	90	120	80	85	85	95	195
Electrician	120	110	135	155	120	95	70	205
Blacksmith	125	145	60	180	205	145	80	125

19. In accordance with the above table, if the average daily   19.___
    pay of the five trades listed above is $47.50, the approxi-
    mate labor cost of work done by the five trades during the
    month of October for Borough 1 is MOST NEARLY
    A. $22,800   B. $23,450   C. $23,750   D. $26,125

20. In accordance with the above table, the Borough which MOST   20.___
    NEARLY made up 22.4% of the total plumbing work force for
    the month of November is Borough
    A. 1   B. 2   C. 3   D. 4

21. In accordance with the above table, the average man days   21.___
    per month per Borough spent on electrical work for all
    Boroughs combined is MOST NEARLY
    A. 120   B. 126   C. 130   D. 136

22. When preparing an estimate for a certain repair job, you   22.___
    determine that $125 worth of materials and 220 man-hours
    are required to complete the job.
    If your man-hour cost is $5.25 per hour, the TOTAL cost
    of this repair job is
       A. $1,030   B. $1,155   C. $1,280   D. $1,405

23. Assume that in determining the total cost of a repair   23.___
    job, a 15% shop cost is to be added to the costs of
    material and labor.
    For a repair job which cost $200 in materials and $600
    in labor, the shop cost is
       A. $30   B. $60   C. $90   D. $120

24. Assume that in quantity purchases, the city receives a   24.___
    discount of 33 1/3%.
    If a one gallon can of paint retails at $5.33 per gallon,
    the cost of 375 gallons of this paint is MOST NEARLY
       A. $1,332.50 B. $1,332.75 C. $1,333.00 D. $1,333.25

25. Assume that eight barrels of cement together weigh a total   25.___
    of 3004 lbs. and 12 oz.
    If there are four bags of cement per barrel, then the
    weight of one bag of cement is MOST NEARLY _____ lbs.
       A. 93.1   B. 93.5   C. 93.9   D. 94.3

26. Lumber is usually sold by the board foot, and a board   26.___
    foot is defined as a board one foot square and one inch
    thick.
    If the price of one board foot of lumber is 18 cents and
    you need 20 feet of lumber 6 inches wide and 1 inch thick,
    the cost of the 20 feet of lumber is
       A. $1.80   B. $2.40   C. $3.60   D. $4.80

27. Assume that a trench is 42" wide, 5' deep, and 100' long.   27.___
    If the unit price of excavating the trench is $35 per
    cubic yard, the cost of excavating the trench is MOST
    NEARLY
       A. $2,275   B. $5,110   C. $7,000   D. $21,000

28. No single activity has a very large effect on the final   28.___
    price of the complete housing structure and, therefore,
    the total cost is not affected appreciably by the price
    policy of any component.
    From the above statement, you may conclude that
       A. we cannot hope for substantial reductions in housing
          costs
       B. the builder must assume responsibility for the high
          cost of construction
       C. a 10% reduction in the cost of materials would result
          in much less than a 10% reduction in the cost of
          housing
       D. federal government financing would reduce the city's
          cost of public housing

29. Four board feet of lumber, listed at $350 per M, will cost 29.___
    A. $3.50   B. $1.40   C. $1.80   D. $4.00

30. The cost of material is approximately 3/8ths of the 30.___
    total cost of a certain job.
    If the total cost of the job is $127.56, then the cost
    of material is MOST NEARLY
    A. $47.83   B. $48.24   C. $48.65   D. $49.06

31. It takes four men six days to do a certain job. 31.___
    Working at the same speed, the number of days it will
    take three men to do this job is
    A. 7   B. 8   C. 9   D. 10

32. A contractor on a large construction project USUALLY 32.___
    receives partial payments based on
    A. estimates of completed work
    B. actual cost of materials delivered and work completed
    C. estimates of material delivered and not paid for by
       the contractor
    D. the breakdown estimate submitted after the contract
       was signed and prorated over the estimated duration
       of the contract

33. In estimating the cost of a reinforced concrete structure, 33.___
    the contractor would be LEAST concerned with
    A. volume of concrete
    B. surface area of forms
    C. pounds of reinforcing steel
    D. type of coarse aggregate

34. Assume that an employee is paid at the rate of $6.25 per 34.___
    hour with time and a half for overtime past 40 hours in
    a week.
    If she works 45 hours in a week, her gross weekly pay is
    A. $285.49   B. $296.88   C. $301.44   D. $325.49

35. Cleaning fluid costs $1.19 a quart. 35.___
    If there is a 10% discount for purchases over 5 gallons,
    how much will 8 gallons cost?
    A. $34.28   B. $38.08   C. $42.28   D. $43.43

KEY (CORRECT ANSWERS)

1. B	11. C	21. B	31. B
2. D	12. B	22. C	32. A
3. B	13. C	23. D	33. D
4. A	14. C	24. A	34. B
5. C	15. A	25. C	35. A
6. B	16. B	26. A	
7. D	17. D	27. A	
8. C	18. C	28. C	
9. D	19. C	29. B	
10. D	20. B	30. A	

TEST 2

DIRECTIONS: Each question or incomplete statement is followed by several suggested answers or completions. Select the one that BEST answers the question or completes the statement. *PRINT THE LETTER OF THE CORRECT ANSWER IN THE SPACE AT THE RIGHT.*

1. When windows are mounted side by side, the vertical piece between them is called the
   A. muntin   B. casement   C. sash   D. mullion

   1.___

2. Approximately how many pounds of 16d nails would be required for 1,000 square feet of floor framing area?
   A. 4-5   B. 7-8   C. 8-10   D. 10-12

   2.___

3. What is represented by the electrical symbol shown at the right?
   A. Transformer   B. Buzzer
   C. Telephone   D. Bell

   3.___

4. Which of the following structures would typically require a relatively higher grade of lumber?
   A. Vertical stud   B. Joist
   C. Column   D. Mud sill

   4.___

5. A dump truck with a capacity of 10-12 cubic yards must load, drive, dump, and reposition itself over a 1-mile haul distance.
   What average amount of time should be estimated for this sequence?
   A. 15 minutes   B. 30 minutes
   C. 1 hour   D. 2 hours

   5.___

6. The stripping of forms that are to be reused should be charged as
   A. common labor   B. masonry labor
   C. carpentry labor   D. material credit

   6.___

7. What type of brick masonry unit is represented by the drawing shown at the right?
   A. Modular
   B. Norwegian
   C. 3 core
   D. Economy

   7.___

8. Which of the following would be a typical thickness of a crushed-rock base course for an area of asphalt paving?
   A. 2"   B. 5"   C. 7"   D. 10"

   8.___

9. Which of the following wood floor materials would be   9.___
   MOST expensive to install?
      A. Unfinished plank   B. Walnut parquet
      C. Maple strip   D. Oak parquet

10. When calculating the air-conditioning needs for a   10.___
    building, a loss factor of ____ should be used for the
    exposure of walls to common heated surfaces.
       A. 2.0   B. 3.5   C. 6.0   D. 7.5

11. Approximately how many linear feet of moldings, door   11.___
    and window trim, handrails, or similar parts can a
    carpenter install in a typical work day?
       A. 100   B. 250   C. 400   D. 500

12. Which of the following constructions is NOT typically   12.___
    found in bathroom lavatories?
       A. Enameled pressed steel   B. Cast iron
       C. Cast ceramic   D. Stainless steel

13. What size reinforcing bar is typically used for masonry 13.___
    walls?
       A. 3   B. 4   C. 7   D. 9

14. Which of the following would NOT be a typical source for 14.___
    a cost-per-square-foot estimate?
       A. Architect   B. Engineer
       C. Appraiser   D. Building contractor

15. Approximately how many stair treads with risers can a   15.___
    carpenter install in an average work day?
       A. 5-8   B. 10-12   C. 15-18   D. 21-25

16. Each of the following materials is commonly used as   16.___
    sheet metal flashing for roof waterproofing EXCEPT
       A. lead   B. galvanized steel
       C. copper   D. zinc

17. The MOST commonly used type of metal lath for wall   17.___
    support is
       A. self-furring   B. flat rib
       C. flat diamond mesh   D. 3/8" rib

18. Approximately how long will it take to install a non-   18.___
    mortised lockset?
       A. 15 minutes   B. 30 minutes
       C. 1 hour   D. 2 hours

19. What is represented by the architectural   19.___
    symbol shown at the right?
       A. Cut stone   B. Concrete block
       C. Rubble stone   D. Brick

20. What type of nails are typically used for installing   20.___
floor sheathing?
    A. 4d   B. 8d   C. 12d   D. 16d

21. Each of the following is considered *finish* electrical   21.___
work EXCEPT
    A. outlet boxes
    B. light fixtures
    C. connection of fixtures to wiring
    D. switches

22. Which component of cost estimating typically presents   22.___
the GREATEST difficulty?
    A. Materials   B. Overhead
    C. Profit   D. Labor

23. Approximately how many hours will it take to install and   23.___
caulk a typical sliding shower door assembly?
    A. 2   B. 4   C. 6   D. 8

24. What is represented by the electrical symbol   24.___
shown at the right?
    A. Single pole switch   B. Lock or key switch
    C. Service weather head   D. Main switch

25. Approximately how many exterior square feet can one   25.___
painter cover, applying a primer coat and two coats of
finish paint, in an average work day?
    A. 100   B. 250   C. 350   D. 500

KEY (CORRECT ANSWERS)

1. D		11. B	
2. B		12. D	
3. C		13. B	
4. B		14. C	
5. B		15. C	
6. C		16. A	
7. A		17. C	
8. B		18. B	
9. B		19. A	
10. B		20. B	

21. A
22. D
23. B
24. A
25. D

TEST 3

DIRECTIONS: Each question or incomplete statement is followed by several suggested answers or completions. Select the one that BEST answers the question or completes the statement. *PRINT THE LETTER OF THE CORRECT ANSWER IN THE SPACE AT THE RIGHT.*

1. Irregular shapes and narrow lites typically reduce the rate of glass installation by ____%.
   A. 10-20   B. 25-35   C. 30-50   D. 55-75   1.___

2. What is represented by the electrical symbol ⎯⋁⎯ shown at the right?
   A. Exposed wiring   B. Fusible element
   C. Three-way switch   D. Circuit breaker   2.___

3. Approximately how many square feet of siding can be installed by a crew in a typical work day?
   A. 250   B. 500   C. 750   D. 1,000   3.___

4. What is the construction term for hinges used on doors?
   A. Gables   B. Butts   C. Hips   D. Plates   4.___

5. Floor joists are typically spaced about ____ apart.
   A. 16"   B. 2 feet   C. 3 feet   D. 4 feet   5.___

6. Which of the following paving materials is generally MOST expensive?
   A. Brick on sand bed   B. Random flagstone
   C. Asphalt   D. Concrete   6.___

7. Approximately how long should it take a 2-person crew to install floor joists for a 100 square-foot area of floor space?
   A. 30 minutes   B. 1 hour
   C. 3 hours   D. 1 work day   7.___

8. A ____ is represented by the mechanical symbol ⎯▷●◁⎯ shown at the right.
   A. pressure-reducing valve   B. motor-operated valve
   C. lock and shield valve   D. globe valve   8.___

9. On average, labor costs for a job will be about ____% of the total job cost.
   A. 15   B. 35   C. 55   D. 85   9.___

10. Most exterior paint averages a coverage of about ____ square feet per gallon.
    A. 100   B. 250   C. 400   D. 550   10.___

11. What type of window includes two sashes which slide   11.___
    vertically?
       A. Double-hung   B. Screen
       C. Casement   D. Sliding

12. Approximately how many linear feet of drywall tape can   12.___
    be applied during an average work day?
       A. 250   B. 400   C. 750   D. 1,000

13. What is used to join lengths of copper pipe?   13.___
       A. Molten solder
       B. Threaded ends and sealer
       C. Nipples
       D. Lead-and-oakum seal

14. Typically, one gallon of prepared wallpaper paste will   14.___
    supply adhesive for _____ full rolls of wall covering.
       A. 8   B. 12   C. 24   D. 36

15. What is represented by the electrical symbol   15.___
    shown at the right?
       A. Range outlet
       B. Wall bracket light fixture
       C. Split-wired receptacle
       D. Special purpose outlet

16. What size is MOST wire used in residential work?   16.___
       A. 6   B. 8   C. 12   D. 16

17. Most fire codes require fire-resistant floor underneath   17.___
    fireplace units which extends to at least _____ inches
    beyond the unit.
       A. 6   B. 12   C. 18   D. 24

18. If a building is constructed without a basement, _____   18.___
    are typically used as footings.
       A. joists   B. staked caissons
       C. grade beams   D. mud sills

19. What is the MOST commonly used size range for flashing   19.___
    and gutter sheet metal?
       A. 8-12   B. 14-18   C. 22-26   D. 24-30

20. Approximately how many square feet of interior wall space   20.___
    can one painter, using a brush, cover in an hour?
       A. 25-50   B. 100   C. 175-200   D. 250

21. Which of the following downspout materials would be   21.___
    MOST expensive?
       A. Copper   B. Aluminum
       C. Zinc   D. Stainless steel

22. What is represented by the mechanical symbol ⊖ shown at the right?   22.___
    A. Expansion valve   B. Floor drain
    C. Shower   D. Scale trap

23. Approximately how much lead (pounds) is required per   23.___
    joint in one sewer line lead-and-oakum seal?
    A. ¼   B. ½   C. 1½   D. 3

24. Which of the following caulking materials is MOST   24.___
    expensive?
    A. Neoprene   B. Butyl
    C. Polyurethane   D. Latex

25. The assembly inside a tank toilet that controls the   25.___
    water supply is the
    A. P trap   B. bell-and-spigot
    C. gating   D. ball cock

———

KEY (CORRECT ANSWERS)

1. C		11. A	
2. B		12. A	
3. A		13. A	
4. B		14. B	
5. A		15. C	
6. D		16. C	
7. C		17. B	
8. D		18. C	
9. A		19. C	
10. C		20. B	

21. A
22. A
23. A
24. B
25. C

WORK SCHEDULING
EXAMINATION SECTION

DIRECTIONS: Each question or incomplete statement is followed by
several suggested answers or completions. Select the
one that BEST answers the question or completes the
statement. *PRINT THE LETTER OF THE CORRECT ANSWER IN
THE SPACE AT THE RIGHT.*

TEST 1

Questions 1-6.

DIRECTIONS: Questions 1 through 6 are to be answered SOLELY on the
basis of the information given in the ELEVATOR OPERATORS'
WORK SCHEDULE shown below.

ELEVATOR OPERATORS' WORK SCHEDULE

Operator	Hours of Work	A.M. Relief Period	Lunch Hour	P.M. Relief Period
Anderson	8:30-4:30	10:20-10:30	12:00-1:00	2:20-2:30
Carter	8:00-4:00	10:10-10:20	11:45-12:45	2:30-2:40
Daniels	9:00-5:00	10:20-10:30	12:30-1:30	3:15-3:25
Grand	9:30-5:30	11:30-11:40	1:00-2:00	4:05-4:15
Jones	7:45-3:45	9:45- 9:55	11:30-12:30	2:05-2:15
Lewis	9:45-5:45	11:40-11:50	1:15-2:15	4:20-4:30
Nance	8:45-4:45	10:50-11:00	12:30-1:30	3:05-3:15
Perkins	8:00-4:00	10:00-10:10	12:00-1:00	2:40-2:50
Russo	7:45-3:45	9:30- 9:40	11:30-12:30	2:10-2:20
Smith	9:45-5:45	11:45-11:55	1:15-2:15	4:05-4:15

1.   The two operators who are on P.M. relief at the SAME time   1.___
are
    A. Anderson and Daniels   B. Carter and Perkins
    C. Jones and Russo   D. Grand and Smith

2.   Of the following, the two operators who have the SAME   2.___
lunch hour are
    A. Anderson and Perkins   B. Daniels and Russo
    C. Grand and Smith   D. Nance and Russo

3.   At 12:15, the number of operators on their lunch hour is   3.___
    A. 3   B. 4   C. 5   D. 6

4.   The operator who has an A.M. relief period right after   4.___
Perkins and a P.M. relief period right before Perkins is
    A. Russo   B. Nance   C. Daniels   D. Carter

5.   The number of operators who are scheduled to be working   5.___
at 4:40 is
    A. 5   B. 6   C. 7   D. 8

6. According to the schedule, it is MOST correct to say that   6. ___
    A. no operator has a relief period during the time that another operator has a lunch hour
    B. each operator has to wait an identical amount of time between the end of lunch and the beginning of P.M. relief period
    C. no operator has a relief period before 9:45 or after 4:00
    D. each operator is allowed a total of 1 hour and 20 minutes for lunch hour and relief periods

TEST 2

Questions 1-7.

DIRECTIONS: Questions 1 through 7 are to be answered SOLELY on the basis of the time sheet and instructions given below.

The following time sheet indicates the times that seven laundry workers arrived and left each day for the week of August 23. The times they arrived for work are shown under the heading *IN*, and the times they left are shown under the heading *OUT*. The letter (P) indicates time which was used for personal business. Time used for this purpose is charged to annual leave. Lunch time is one-half hour from noon to 12:30 P.M. and is not accounted for on this time record.

The employees on this shift are scheduled to work from 8:00 A.M. to 4:00 P.M. Lateness is charged to annual leave. Reporting after 8:00 A.M. is considered late.

	MON. AM IN	MON. PM OUT	TUES. AM IN	TUES. PM OUT	WED. AM IN	WED. PM OUT	THURS. AM IN	THURS. PM OUT	FRI. AM IN	FRI. PM OUT
Baxter	7:50	4:01	7:49	4:07	8:00	4:07	8:20	4:00	7:42	4:03
Gardner	8:02	4:00	8:20	4:00	8:05	3:30(P)	8:00	4:03	8:00	4:07
Clements	8:00	4:04	8:03	4:01	7:59	4:00	7:54	4:06	7:59	4:00
Tompkins	7:56	4:00	Annual leave		8:00	4:07	7:59	4:00	8:00	4:01
Wagner	8:04	4:03	7:40	4:00	7:53	4:04	8:00	4:09	7:53	4:00
Patterson	8:00	2:30(P)	8:15	4:04	Sick leave		7:45	4:00	7:59	4:04
Cunningham	7:43	4:02	7:50	4:00	7:59	4:02	8:00	4:10	8:00	4:00

1. Which one of the following laundry workers did NOT have   1. ___
   any time charged to annual leave or sick leave during the week?
    A. Gardner   B. Clements   C. Tompkins   D. Cunningham

2. On which day did ALL the laundry workers arrive on time?   2.___
      A. Monday   B. Wednesday C. Thursday   D. Friday

3. Which of the following laundry workers used time to take   3.___
   care of personal business?
      A. Baxter and Clements   B. Patterson and Cunningham
      C. Gardner and Patterson   D. Wagner and Tompkins

4. How many laundry workers were late on Monday?   4.___
      A. 1   B. 2   C. 3   D. 4

5. Which one of the following laundry workers arrived late   5.___
   on three of the five days?
      A. Baxter   B. Gardner   C. Wagner   D. Patterson

6. The percentage of laundry workers reporting to work late   6.___
   on Tuesday is MOST NEARLY
      A. 15%   B. 25%   C. 45%   D. 50%

7. The percentage of laundry workers that were absent for an   7.___
   entire day during the week is MOST NEARLY
      A. 6%   B. 9%   C. 15%   D. 30%

———

TEST 3

Questions 1-9.

DIRECTIONS: Questions 1 through 9 are to be answered SOLELY on the
              basis of the following information and timesheet given
              below.

     The following is a foreman's timesheet for his crew for one week.
The hours worked each day or the reason the man was off on that day
are shown on the sheet. *R* means rest day. *A* means annual leave.
S means sick leave. Where a man worked only part of a day, both the
number of hours worked and the number of hours taken off are entered.
The reason for absence is entered in parentheses next to the number
of hours taken off.

Name	Saturday	Sunday	Monday	Tuesday	Wednesday	Thursday	Friday
Smith	R	R	7	7	7	3 4(A)	7
Jones	R	7	7	7	7	7	R
Green	R	R	7	7	S	S	S
White	R	R	7	7	A	7	7
Doe	7	7	7	7	7	R	R
Brown	R	R	A	7	7	7	7
Black	R	R	S	7	7	7	7
Reed	R	R	7	7	7	7	S
Roe	R	R	A	7	7	7	7
Lane	7	R	R	7	7	A	S

3

1. The caretaker who worked EXACTLY 21 hours during the week   1.___
   is
      A. Lane   B. Roe   C. Smith   D. White

2. The TOTAL number of hours worked by all caretakers during   2.___
   the week is
      A. 268   B. 276   C. 280   D. 288

3. The two days of the week on which MOST caretakers were off   3.___
   are
      A. Thursday and Friday   B. Friday and Saturday
      C. Saturday and Sunday   D. Sunday and Monday

4. The day on which three caretakers were off on sick leave is   4.___
      A. Monday   B. Friday   C. Saturday   D. Sunday

5. The two workers who took LEAST time off during the week are   5.___
      A. Doe and Reed   B. Jones and Doe
      C. Reed and Smith   D. Smith and Jones

6. The caretaker who worked the LEAST number of hours during   6.___
   the week is
      A. Brown   B. Green   C. Lane   D. Roe

7. The caretakers who did NOT work on Thursday are   7.___
      A. Doe, White, and Smith
      B. Green, Doe, and Lane
      C. Green, Doe, and Smith
      D. Green, Lane, and Smith

8. The day on which one caretaker worked ONLY 3 hours is   8.___
      A. Friday   B. Saturday   C. Thursday   D. Wednesday

9. The day on which ALL caretakers worked is   9.___
      A. Monday   B. Thursday   C. Tuesday   D. Wednesday

4

TEST 4

Questions 1-6.

DIRECTIONS: Questions 1 through 6 are to be answered SOLELY on the
basis of the table below which shows the initial
requests made by staff for vacation. It is to be used
with the RULES AND GUIDELINES to make the decisions
and judgments called for in each of the questions.

			Accumulated Annual Leave Days	
Name	Work Assignment	Date Appointed		Vacation Periods Requested
DeMarco	MVO	Mar. 1983	25	May 3-21; Oct. 25-Nov. 5
Moore	Dispatcher	Dec. 1977	32	May 24-June 4; July 12-16
Kingston	MVO	Apr. 1987	28	May 24-June 11; Feb. 7-25
Green	MVO	June 1986	26	June 7-18; Sept. 6-24
Robinson	MVO	July 1988	30	June 28-July 9; Nov. 15-26
Reilly	MVO	Oct. 1989	23	July 5-9; Jan. 31-Mar. 3
Stevens	MVO	Sept.1976	31	July 5-23; Oct. 4-29
Costello	MVO	Sept.1978	31	July 5-30; Oct. 4-22
Maloney	Dispatcher	Aug. 1972	35	July 5-Aug. 6; Nov. 1-5
Hughes	Director	Feb. 1970	38	July 26-Sept. 3
Lord	MVO	Jan. 1990	20	Aug. 9-27; Feb. 7-25
Diaz	MVO	Dec. 1989	28	Aug. 9-Sept. 10
Krimsky	MVO	May 1986	22	Oct. 18-22; Nov. 22-Dec. 1(

VACATION REQUESTS FOR THE ONE YEAR PERIOD FROM MAY 1, YEAR X THROUGH APRIL 30, YEAR Y

RULES AND GUIDELINES

1. The two Dispatchers cannot be on vacation at the same time, nor
    can a Dispatcher be on vacation at the same time as the Director.
2. For the period June 1 through September 30, not more than three
    MVO's can be on vacation at the same time.
3. For the period October 1 through May 31, not more than two MVO's
    at a time can be on vacation.
4. In cases where the same vacation time is requested by too many
    employees for all of them to be given the time under the rules,
    the requests of those who have worked the longest will be granted.
5. No employee may take more leave days than the number of annual
    leave days accumulated and shown in the table.
6. All vacation periods shown in the table and described in the
    questions below begin on a Monday and end on a Friday.
7. Employees work a five-day week (Monday through Friday). They are
    off weekends and holidays with no charges to leave balances. When
    a holiday falls on a Saturday or Sunday, employees are given the
    following Monday off without charge to annual leave.
8. Holidays: May 31   October 25   January 1
                 July 4   November 2   February 12
                 September 6   November 25   February 21
                 October 11   December 25   February 21

9. An employee shall be given any part of his initial requests that is permissible under the above rules and shall have first right to it despite any further adjustment of schedule.

---

1. Until adjustments in the vacation schedule can be made, the vacation dates that can be approved for Krimsky are
   A. Oct. 18-22; Nov. 22-Dec. 10
   B. Oct. 18-22; Nov. 29-Dec. 10
   C. Oct. 18-22 *only*
   D. Nov. 22-Dec. 10 *only*

2. Until adjustments in the vacation schedule can be made, the vacation dates that can be approved for Maloney are
   A. July 5-Aug. 6; Nov. 1-5
   B. July 5-23; Nov. 1-5
   C. July 5-9; Nov. 1-5
   D. Nov. 1-5 *only*

3. According to the table, Lord wants a vacation in August and another in February.
   Until adjustments in the vacation schedule can be made, he can be allowed to take _____ of the August vacation and _____ of the February vacation.
   A. all; none   B. all; almost half
   C. almost all; almost half   D. almost half; all

4. Costello cannot be given all the vacation he has requested because
   A. the MVO's who have more seniority than he has have requested time he wishes
   B. he does not have enough accumulated annual leave
   C. a dispatcher is applying for vacation at the same time as Costello
   D. there are five people who want vacation in July

5. According to the table, how many leave days will DeMarco be charged for his vacation from October 25 through November 5?
   A. 10   B. 9   C. 8   D. 7

6. How many leave days will Moore use if he uses the requested vacation allowable to him under the rules?
   A. 9   B. 10   C. 14   D. 15

TEST 5

Questions 1-8.

DIRECTIONS: Questions 1 through 8 are to be answered SOLELY on the basis of Charts I, II, III, and IV. Assume that you are the supervisor of Operators R, S, T, U, V, W, and X, and it is your responsibility to schedule their lunch hours.

The charts each represent a possible scheduling of lunch hours during a lunch period from 11:30 - 2:00. An operator-hour is one hour of time spent by one operator. Each box on the chart represents one half-hour. The boxes marked *L* represent the time when each operator is scheduled to have her lunch hour. For example, in Chart I, next to Operator R, the boxes for 11:30 - 12:00 and 12:00 - 12:30 are marked *L*. This means that Operator R is scheduled to have her lunch hour from 11:30 to 12:30.

I

	11:30-12:00	12:00-12:30	12:30-1:00	1:00-1:30	1:30-2:00
R	L	L			
S		L	L		
T		L	L		
U			L	L	
V			L	L	
W				L	L
X				L	L

II

	11:30-12:00	12:00-12:30	12:30-1:00	1:00-1:30	1:30-2:00
R				L	L
S		L	L		
T	L	L			
U		L	L		
V				L	L
W				L	L
X			L	L	

III

	11:30-12:00	12:00-12:30	12:30-1:00	1:00-1:30	1:30-2:00
R	L	L			
S				L	L
T	L	L			
U			L	L	
V	L	L			
W			L	L	
X			L	L	

IV

	11:30-12:00	12:00-12:30	12:30-1:00	1:00-1:30	1:30-2:00
R	L	L			
S	L	L			
T		L	L		
U			L	L	
V				L	L
W				L	L
X			L	L	

1. If, under the schedule represented in Chart II, Operator R has her lunch hour changed to 12:30-1:30, that leaves how many operator-hours of phone coverage from 1:00-2:00?
   A. 2   B. 2½   C. 3   D. 4½

2. If Operator S asks you whether she and Operator T may have the same lunch hour, you could accommodate her by using the schedule in Chart
   A. I   B. II   C. III   D. IV

3. From past experience you know that the part of the lunch period when the phones are busiest is from 12:30-1:30. Which chart shows the BEST phone coverage from 12:30 to 1:30?
   A. I   B. II   C. III   D. IV

7

4. At least three operators have the same lunch hour according   4.___
    to Chart(s)
        A. II and III   B. II and IV
        C. III *only*   D. IV *only*

5. Which chart would provide the POOREST phone coverage   5.___
    during the period 12:00-1:30, based on total number of
    operator-hours from 12:00 to 1:30?
        A. I   B. II   C. III   D. IV

6. Which chart would make it possible for U, W, and X to   6.___
    have the same lunch hour?
        A. I   B. II   C. III   D. IV

7. The portion of the lunch period during which the telephones   7.___
    are least busy is 11:30-12:30.
    Which chart is MOST likely to have been designed with that
    fact in mind?
        A. I   B. II   C. III   D. IV

8. Assume that you have decided to use Chart IV to schedule   8.___
    your operators' lunch hours on a specific day. Operator T
    asks you if she can have her lunch hour changed to 1:00-
    2:00.
    If you grant her request, how many operators will be working
    during the period 12:00 to 12:30?
        A. 1   B. 2   C. 4   D. 5

TEST 6

Questions 1-13.

DIRECTIONS: Questions 1 through 13 consist of a statement. You are
to indicate whether the statement is TRUE (T) or FALSE (F)
*PRINT THE LETTER OF THE CORRECT ANSWER IN THE SPACE AT
THE RIGHT.* Questions 1 through 13 are to be answered
SOLELY on the basis of the information given in the
table below.

DEPARTMENT OF FERRIES
ATTENDANTS WORK ASSIGNMENT - JULY 1983

Name	Year Employed	Ferry Assigned	Hours of Work	Lunch Period	Days Off
Adams	1979	Hudson	7 AM - 3 PM	11-12	Fri. and Sat.
Baker	1972	Monroe	7 AM - 3 PM	11-12	Sun. and Mon.
Gunn	1975	Troy	8 AM - 4 PM	12-1	Fri. and Sat.
Hahn	1969	Erie	9 AM - 5 PM	1-2	Sat. and Sun.
King	1978	Albany	7 AM - 3 PM	11-12	Sun. and Mon.
Nash	1973	Hudson	11 AM - 7 PM	3-4	Sun. and Mon.
Olive	1983	Fulton	10 AM - 6 PM	2-3	Sat. and Sun.
Queen	1982	Albany	11 AM - 7 PM	3-4	Fri. and Sat.
Rose	1970	Troy	11 AM - 7 PM	3-4	Sun. and Mon.
Smith	1971	Monroe	10 AM - 6 PM	2-3	Fri. and Sat.

1. The chart shows that there are only five (5) ferries being used. 1.___

2. The attendant who has been working the LONGEST time is Rose. 2.___

3. The <u>Troy</u> has one more attendant assigned to it than the Erie. 3.___

4. Two (2) attendants are assigned to work from 10 P.M. to 6 A.M. 4.___

5. According to the chart, no more than one attendant was hired in any year. 5.___

6. The NEWEST employee is Olive. 6.___

7. There are as many attendants on the 7 to 3 shift as on the 11 to 7 shift. 7.___

8. MOST of the attendants have their lunch either between 12 and 1 or 2 and 3. 8.___

9. All the employees work four (4) hours before they go to lunch. 9.___

10. On the <u>Hudson</u>, Adams goes to lunch when Nash reports to work. 10.___

11. All the attendants who work on the 7 to 3 shift are off on Saturday and Sunday. 11.___

12. All the attendants have either a Saturday or Sunday as one of their days off. 12.___

13. At least two (2) attendants are assigned to each ferry. 13.___

KEY (CORRECT ANSWERS)

TEST 1	TEST 2	TEST 3	TEST 4	TEST 5	TEST 6
1. D	1. D	1. A	1. D	1. D	1. F
2. A	2. D	2. B	2. B	2. A	2. F
3. C	3. C	3. C	3. A	3. B	3. T
4. D	4. B	4. B	4. B	4. A	4. F
5. A	5. B	5. B	5. C	5. A	5. T
6. D	6. C	6. B	6. A	6. C	6. T
	7. D	7. B		7. C	7. T
		8. C		8. D	8. F
		9. C			9. T
					10. T
					11. F
					12. T
					13. F

EXAMINATION SECTION

TEST 1

DIRECTIONS: Each question or incomplete statement is followed by several suggested answers or completions. Select the one that BEST answers the question or completes the statement. *PRINT THE LETTER OF THE CORRECT ANSWER IN THE SPACE AT THE RIGHT.*

1. Of the following, the one MOST important quality required of a good supervisor is
    A. ambition
    B. leadership
    C. friendliness
    D. popularity

1.___

2. It is often said that a supervisor can delegate authority but never responsibility.
This means MOST NEARLY that
    A. a supervisor must do his own work if he expects it to be done properly
    B. a supervisor can assign someone else to do his work, but in the last analysis, the supervisor himself must take the blame for any actions followed
    C. authority and responsibility are two separate things that cannot be borne by the same person
    D. it is better for a supervisor never to delegate his authority

2.___

3. One of your men who is a habitual complainer asks you to grant him a minor privilege.
Before granting or denying such a request, you should consider
    A. the merits of the case
    B. that it is good for group morale to grant a request of this nature
    C. the man's seniority
    D. that to deny such a request will lower your standing with the men

3.___

4. A supervisory practice on the part of a foreman which is MOST likely to lead to confusion and inefficiency is for him to
    A. give orders verbally directly to the man assigned to the job
    B. issue orders only in writing
    C. follow up his orders after issuing them
    D. relay his orders to the men through co-workers

4.___

5. It would be POOR supervision on a foreman's part if he
    A. asked an experienced maintainer for his opinion on the method of doing a special job
    B. make it a policy to avoid criticizing a man in front of his co-workers
    C. consulted his assistant supervisor on unusual problems
    D. allowed a cooling-off period of several days before giving one of his men a deserved reprimand

5.___

6. Of the following behavior characteristics of a supervisor,   6.___
the one that is MOST likely to lower the morale of the men
he supervises is
    A. diligence   B. favoritism
    C. punctuality   D. thoroughness

7. Of the following, the BEST method of getting an employee   7.___
who is not working up to his capacity to produce more work
is to
    A. have another employee criticize his production
    B. privately criticize his production but encourage him
       to produce more
    C. criticize his production before his associates
    D. criticize his production and threaten to fire him

8. Of the following, the BEST thing for a supervisor to do   8.___
when a subordinate has done a very good job is to
    A. tell him to take it easy
    B. praise his work
    C. reduce his workload
    D. say nothing because he may become conceited

9. Your orders to your crew are MOST likely to be followed if   9.___
you
    A. explain the reasons for these orders
    B. warn that all violators will be punished
    C. promise easy assignments to those who follow these
       orders best
    D. say that they are for the good of the department

10. In order to be a good supervisor, you should   10.___
    A. impress upon your men that you demand perfection in
       their work at all times
    B. avoid being blamed for your crew's mistakes
    C. impress your superior with your ability
    D. see to it that your men get what they are entitled to

11. In giving instructions to a crew, you should   11.___
    A. speak in as loud a tone as possible
    B. speak in a coaxing, persuasive manner
    C. speak quietly, clearly, and courteously
    D. always use the word *please* when giving instructions

12. Of the following factors, the one which is LEAST important   12.___
in evaluating an employee and his work is his
    A. dependability   B. quantity of work done
    C. quality of work done   D. education and training

13. When a District Superintendent first assumes his command,   13.___
it is LEAST important for him at the beginning to observe
    A. how his equipment is designed and its adaptability
    B. how to reorganize the district for greater efficiency
    C. the capabilities of the men in the district
    D. the methods of operation being employed

14. When making an inspection of one of the buildings under   14.___
    your supervision, the BEST procedure to follow in making
    a record of the inspection is to
    A. return immediately to the office and write a report
       from memory
    B. write down all the important facts during or as soon
       as you complete the inspection
    C. fix in your mind all important facts so that you can
       repeat them from memory if necessary
    D. fix in your mind all important facts so that you can
       make out your report at the end of the day

15. Assume that your superior has directed you to make certain 15.___
    changes in your established procedure. After using this
    modified procedure on several occasions, you find that the
    original procedure was distinctly superior and you wish to
    return to it.
    You should
    A. let your superior find this out for himself
    B. simply change back to the original procedure
    C. compile definite data and information to prove your
       case to your superior
    D. persuade one of the more experienced workers to take
       this matter up with your superior

16. An inspector visited a large building under construction.   16.___
    He inspected the soil lines at 9 A.M., water lines at
    10 A.M., fixtures at 11 A.M., and did his office work in
    the afternoon. He followed the same pattern daily for
    weeks.
    This procedure was
    A. *good*; because it was methodical and he did not miss
       anything
    B. *good*; because it gave equal time to all phases of the
       plumbing
    C. *bad*; because not enough time was devoted to fixtures
    D. *bad*; because the tradesmen knew when the inspection
       would occur

17. Assume that one of the foremen in a training course,   17.___
    which you are conducting, proposes a poor solution for a
    maintenance problem.
    Of the following, the BEST course of action for you to
    take is to
    A. accept the solution tentatively and correct it during
       the next class meeting
    B. point out all the defects of this proposed solution
       and wait until somebody thinks of a better solution
    C. try to get the class to reject this proposed solution
       and develop a better solution
    D. let the matter pass since somebody will present a
       better solution as the class work proceeds

18. As a supervisor, you should be seeking ways to improve   18.___
    the efficiency of shop operations by means such as
    changing established work procedures.
    The following are offered as possible actions that you
    should consider in changing established work procedures:
      I. Make changes only when your foremen agree to them
     II. Discuss changes with your supervisor before putting
         them into practice
    III. Standardize any operation which is performed on a
         continuing basis
     IV. Make changes quickly and quietly in order to avoid
         dissent
      V. Secure expert guidance before instituting unfamiliar
         procedures

    Of the following suggested answers, the one that describes
    the actions to be taken to change established work proce-
    dures is
      A. I, IV, and V *only*   B. II, III, and V *only*
      C. III, IV, and V *only*   D. All of the above

19. A supervisor determined that a foreman, without informing   19.___
    his superior, delegated responsibility for checking time
    cards to a member of his gang. The supervisor then called
    the foreman into his office where he reprimanded the
    foreman.
    This action of the supervisor in reprimanding the foreman
    was
      A. *proper*;because the checking of time cards is the
         foreman's responsibility and should not be delegated
      B. *proper*;because the foreman did not ask the supervisor
         for permission to delegate responsibility
      C. *improper*;because the foreman may no longer take the
         initiative in solving future problems
      D. *improper*;because the supervisor is interfering in a
         function which is not his responsibility

20. A capable supervisor should check all operations under   20.___
    his control.
    Of the following, the LEAST important reason for doing
    this is to make sure that
      A. operations are being performed as scheduled
      B. he personally observes all operations at all times
      C. all the operations are still needed
      D. his manpower is being utilized efficiently

21. A supervisor makes it a practice to apply fair and firm   21.___
    discipline in all cases of rule infractions, including
    those of a minor nature.
    This practice should PRIMARILY be considered
      A. *bad*;since applying discipline for minor violations
         is a waste of time
      B. *good*;because not applying discipline for minor infrac-
         tions can lead to a more serious erosion of discipline
      C. *bad*;because employees do not like to be disciplined
         for minor violations of the rules
      D. *good*;because violating any rule can cause a dangerous
         situation to occur

22. A maintainer would PROPERLY consider it poor supervisory practice for a foreman to consult with him on
    A. which of several repair jobs should be scheduled first
    B. how to cope with personal problems at home
    C. whether the neatness of his headquarters can be improved
    D. how to express a suggestion which the maintainer plans to submit formally
    22.___

23. Assume that you have determined that the work of one of your foremen and the men he supervises is consistently behind schedule. When you discuss this situation with the foreman, he tells you that his men are poor workers and then complains that he must spend all of his time checking on their work.
    23.___

The following actions are offered for your consideration as possible ways of solving the problem of poor performance of the foreman and his men:
    I. Review the work standards with the foreman and determine whether they are realistic
    II. Tell the foreman that you will recommend him for the foreman's training course for retraining
    III. Ask the foreman for the names of the maintainers and then replace them as soon as possible
    IV. Tell the foreman that you expect him to meet a satisfactory level of performance
    V. Tell the foreman to insist that his men work overtime to catch up to the schedule
    VI. Tell the foreman to review the type and amount of training he has given the maintainers
    VII. Tell the foreman that he will be out of a job if he does not produce on schedule
    VIII. Avoid all criticism of the foreman and his methods

Which of the following suggested answers CORRECTLY lists the proper actions to be taken to solve the problem of poor performance of the foreman and his men?
    A. I, II, IV, and VI *only*
    B. I, III, V, and VII *only*
    C. II, III, VI, and VIII *only*
    D. IV, V, VI, and VIII *only*

24. When a conference or a group discussion is tending to turn into a *bull session* without constructive purpose, the BEST action to take is to
    A. reprimand the leader of the *bull session*
    B. redirect the discussion to the business at hand
    C. dismiss the meeting and reschedule it for another day
    D. allow the *bull session* to continue
    24.___

25. Assume that you have been assigned responsibility for a program in which a high production rate is mandatory. From past experience, you know that your foremen do not perform equally well in the various types of jobs given to them.
    25.___

Which of the following methods should you use in selecting foremen for the specific types of work involved in the program?
   A. Leave the method of selecting foremen to your super-
      visor
   B. Assign each foreman to the work he does best
   C. Allow each foreman to choose his own job
   D. Assign each foreman to a job which will permit him
      to improve his own abilities

———

KEY (CORRECT ANSWERS)

1. B		11. C
2. B		12. D
3. A		13. B
4. D		14. B
5. D		15. C
6. B		16. D
7. B		17. C
8. B		18. B
9. A		19. A
10. D		20. B

21. B
22. A
23. A
24. B
25. B

———

TEST 2

1. A foreman who is familiar with modern management principles should know that the one of the following requirements of an administrator which is LEAST important is his ability to
   A. coordinate work
   B. plan, organize, and direct the work under his control
   C. cooperate with others
   D. perform the duties of the employees under his jurisdiction

   1.___

2. When subordinates request his advice in solving problems encountered in their work, a certain chief occasionally answers the request by first asking the subordinate what he thinks should be done.
   This action by the chief is, on the whole,
   A. *desirable* because it stimulates subordinates to give more thought to the solution of problems encountered
   B. *undesirable* because it discourages subordinates from asking questions
   C. *desirable* because it discourages subordinates from asking questions
   D. *undesirable* because it undermines the confidence of subordinates in the ability of their supervisor

   2.___

3. Of the following factors that may be considered by a unit head in dealing with the tardy subordinate, the one which should be given LEAST consideration is the
   A. frequency with which the employee is tardy
   B. effect of the employee's tardiness upon the work of other employees
   C. willingness of the employee to work overtime when necessary
   D. cause of the employee's tardiness

   3.___

4. The MOST important requirement of a good inspectional report is that it should be
   A. properly addressed   B. lengthy
   C. clear and brief   D. spelled correctly

   4.___

5. Building superintendents frequently inquire about departmental inspectional procedures.
   Of the following, it is BEST to
   A. advise them to write to the department for an official reply
   B. refuse as the inspectional procedure is a restricted matter
   C. briefly explain the procedure to them
   D. avoid the inquiry by changing the subject

   5.___

6. Reprimanding a crew member before other workers is a
    A. *good practice*; the reprimand serves as a warning to the other workers
    B. *bad practice*; people usually resent criticism made in public
    C. *good practice*; the other workers will realize that the supervisor is fair
    D. *bad practice*; the other workers will take sides in the dispute

6.___

7. Of the following actions, the one which is LEAST likely to promote good work is for the group leader to
    A. praise workers for doing a good job
    B. call attention to the opportunities for promotion for better workers
    C. threaten to recommend discharge of workers who are below standard
    D. put into practice any good suggestion made by crew members

7.___

8. A supervisor notices that a member of his crew has skipped a routine step in his job.
Of the following, the BEST action for the supervisor to take is to
    A. promptly question the worker about the incident
    B. immediately assign another man to complete the job
    C. bring up the incident the next time the worker asks for a favor
    D. say nothing about the incident but watch the worker carefully in the future

8.___

9. Assume you have been told to show a new worker how to operate a piece of equipment.
Your FIRST step should be to
    A. ask the worker if he has any questions about the equipment
    B. permit the worker to operate the equipment himself while you carefully watch to prevent damage
    C. demonstrate the operation of the equipment for the worker
    D. have the worker read an instruction booklet on the maintenance of the equipment

9.___

10. Whenever a new man was assigned to his crew, the supervisor would introduce him to all other crew members, take him on a tour of the plant, tell him about bus schedules and places to eat.
This practice is
    A. *good*; the new man is made to feel welcome
    B. *bad*; supervisors should not interfere in personal matters
    C. *good*; the new man knows that he can bring his personal problems to the supervisor
    D. *bad*; work time should not be spent on personal matters

10.___

11. The MOST important factor in successful leadership is   11.___
    the ability to
    A. obtain instant obedience to all orders
    B. establish friendly personal relations with crew members
    C. avoid disciplining crew members
    D. make crew members want to do what should be done

12. Explaining the reasons for departmental procedure to   12.___
    workers tends to
    A. waste time which should be used for productive purposes
    B. increase their interest in their work
    C. make them more critical of departmental procedures
    D. confuse them

13. If you want a job done well, do it yourself.   13.___
    For a supervisor to follow this advice would be
    A. *good*; a supervisor is responsible for the work of his
       crew
    B. *bad*; a supervisor should train his men, not do their
       work
    C. *good*; a supervisor should be skilled in all jobs
       assigned to his crew
    D. *bad*; a supervisor loses respect when he works with his
       hands

14. When a supervisor discovers a mistake in one of the jobs   14.___
    for which his crew is responsible, it is MOST important
    for him to find out
    A. whether anybody else knows about the mistake
    B. who was to blame for the mistake
    C. how to prevent similar mistakes in the future
    D. whether similar mistakes occurred in the past

15. A supervisor who has to explain a new procedure to his   15.___
    crew should realize that questions from the crew USUALLY
    show that they
    A. are opposed to the new procedure
    B. are completely confused by the explanation
    C. need more training in the new procedure
    D. are interested in the explanation

16. A GOOD way for a supervisor to retain the confidence of   16.___
    his or her employees is to
    A. say as little as possible
    B. check work frequently
    C. make no promises unless they will be fulfilled
    D. never hesitate in giving an answer to any question

17. Good supervision is ESSENTIALLY a matter of   17.___
    A. patience in supervising workers
    B. care in selecting workers
    C. skill in human relations
    D. fairness in disciplining workers

18. It is MOST important for an employee who has been assigned   18.____
a monotonous task to
    A. perform this task before doing other work
    B. ask another employee to help
    C. perform this task only after all other work has been
       completed
    D. take measures to prevent mistakes in performing the
       task

19. One of your employees has violated a minor agency regula-   19.____
tion.
The FIRST thing you should do is
    A. warn the employee that you will have to take disci-
       plinary action if it should happen again
    B. ask the employee to explain his or her actions
    C. inform your supervisor and wait for advice
    D. write a memo describing the incident and place it in
       the employee's personnel file

20. One of your employees tells you that he feels you give   20.____
him much more work than the other employees, and he is
having trouble meeting your deadlines.
You should
    A. ask if he has been under a lot of non-work related
       stress lately
    B. review his recent assignments to determine if he is
       correct
    C. explain that this is a busy time, but you are dividing
       the work equally
    D. tell him that he is the most competent employee and
       that is why he receives more work

21. A supervisor assigns one of his crew to complete a portion   21.____
of a job. A short time later, the supervisor notices that
the portion has not been completed.
Of the following, the BEST way for the supervisor to
handle this is to
    A. ask the crew member why he has not completed the
       assignment
    B. reprimand the crew member for not obeying orders
    C. assign another crew member to complete the assignment
    D. complete the assignment himself

22. Suppose that a member of your crew complains that you are   22.____
playing favorites in assigning work.
Of the following, the BEST method of handling the complaint
is to
    A. deny it and refuse to discuss the matter with the worker
    B. take the opportunity to tell the worker what is wrong
       with his work
    C. ask the worker for examples to prove his point and try
       to clear up any misunderstanding
    D. promise to be more careful in making assignments in
       the future

23. A member of your crew comes to you with a complaint.   23.____
    After discussing the matter with him, it is clear that
    you have convinced him that his complaint was not justified.
    At this point, you should
       A. permit him to drop the matter
       B. make him admit his error
       C. pretend to see some justification in his complaint
       D. warn him against making unjustified complaints

24. Suppose that a supervisor has in his crew an older man   24.____
    who works rather slowly. In other respects, this man is
    a good worker; he is seldom absent, works carefully, never
    loafs, and is cooperative.
    The BEST way for the supervisor to handle this worker is to
       A. try to get him to work faster and less carefully
       B. give him the most disagreeable job
       C. request that he be given special training
       D. permit him to work at his own speed

25. Suppose that a member of your crew comes to you with a   25.____
    suggestion he thinks will save time in doing a job. You
    realize immediately that it won't work.
    Under these circumstances, your BEST action would be to
       A. thank the worker for the suggestion and forget about it
       B. explain to the worker why you think it won't work
       C. tell the worker to put the suggestion in writing
       D. ask the other members of your crew to criticize the
          suggestion

KEY (CORRECT ANSWERS)

1. D		11. D	
2. A		12. B	
3. C		13. B	
4. C		14. C	
5. C		15. D	
6. B		16. C	
7. C		17. C	
8. A		18. D	
9. C		19. B	
10. A		20. B	

21. A
22. C
23. A
24. D
25. B

SUPERVISION STUDY GUIDE

Social science has developed information about groups and leadership in general and supervisor-employee relationships in particular. Since organizational effectiveness is closely linked to the ability of supervisors to direct the activities of employees, these findings are important to executives everywhere.

IS A SUPERVISOR A LEADER?

First-line supervisors are found in all large business and government organizations. They are the men at the base of an organizational hierarchy. Decisions made by the head of the organization reach them through a network of intermediate positions. They are frequently referred to as part of the management team, but their duties seldom seem to support this description.

A supervisor of clerks, tax collectors, meat inspectors, or securities analysts is not charged with budget preparation. He cannot hire or fire the employees in his own unit on his say-so. He does not administer programs which require great planning, coordinating, or decision making.

Then what is he? He is the man who is directly in charge of a group of employees doing productive work for a business or government agency. If the work requires the use of machines, the men he supervises operate them. If the work requires the writing of reports, the men he supervises write them. He is expected to maintain a productive flow of work without creating problems which higher levels of management must solve. But is he a leader?

To carry out a specific part of an agency's mission, management creates a unit, staffs it with a group of employees and designates a supervisor to take charge of them. Management directs what this unit shall do, from time to time changes directions, and often indicates what the group should not do. Management presumably creates status for the supervisor by giving him more pay, a title, and special priviledges.

Management asks a supervisor to get his workers to attain organizational goals, including the desired quantity and quality of production. Supposedly, he has authority to enable him to achieve this objective. Management at least assumes that by establishing the status of the supervisor's position it has created sufficient authority to enable him to achieve these goals -- not his goals, nor necessarily the group's, but management's goals.

In addition, supervision includes writing reports, keeping records of membership in a higher-level administrative group, industrial engineering, safety engineering, editorial duties, housekeeping duties, etc. The supervisor as a member of an organizational network, must be responsible to the changing demands of the management above him. At the same time, he must be responsive to the demands of the work group of which he is a member. He is placed in the difficult position of communicating and implementing new decisions, changed programs and revised production quotas for his work group, although he may have had little part in developing them.

It follows, then, that supervision has a special characteristic: achievement of goals, previously set by management, through the efforts of others. It is in this feature of the supervisor's job that we find the role of a leader in the sense of the following definition: *A leader is that person who <u>most</u> effectively influences group activities toward goal setting and <u>goal</u> achievements.*

This definition is broad. It covers both leaders in groups that come together voluntarily and in those brought together through a work assignment in a factory, store, or government agency. In the natural group, the authority necessary to attain goals is determined by the group membership and is granted by them. In the working group, it is apparent that the establishment of a supervisory position creates a predisposition on the part of employees to accept the authority of the occupant of that position. We cannot, however, assume that mere occupancy confers authority sufficient to assure the accomplishment of an organization's goals.

Supervision is different, then, from leadership. The supervisor is expected to fulfill the role of leader but without obtaining a grant of authority from the group he supervises. The supervisor is expected to influence the group in the achieving of goals but is often handicapped by having little influence on the organizational process by which goals are set. The supervisor, because he works in an organizational setting, has the burdens of additional organizational duties and restrictions and requirements arising out of the fact that his position is subordinate to a hierarchy of higher-level supervisors. These differences between leadership and supervision are reflected in our definition: *Supervision is basically a leadership role, in a formal organization, which has as its objective the effective influencing of other employees.*

Even though these differences between supervision and leadership exist, a significant finding of experimenters in this field is that supervisors <u>must</u> be leaders to be successful.

The problem is: How can a supervisor exercise leadership in an organizational setting? We might say that the supervisor is expected to be a natural leader in a situation which does not come about naturally. His situation becomes really difficult in an organization which is more eager to make its supervisors into followers rather than leaders.

LEADERSHIP: NATURAL AND ORGANIZATIONAL

Leadership, in its usual sense of *natural* leadership, and supervision are not the same. In some cases, leadership embraces broader powers and functions than supervision; in other cases, supervision embraces more than leadership. This is true both because of the organization and technical aspects of the supervisor's job and because of the relatively freer setting and inherent authority of the natural leader.

The natural leader usually has much more authority and influence than the supervisor. Group members not only follow his command but prefer it that way. The employee, however, can appeal the supervisor's commands to his union or to the supervisor's superior or to the personnel office. These intercessors represent restrictions on the supervisor's power to lead.

The natural leader can gain greater membership involvement in the group's objectives, and he can change the objectives of the group. The supervisor can attempt to gain employee support only for management's objectives; he cannot set other objectives. In these instances leadership is broader than supervision.

The natural leader must depend upon whatever skills are available when seeking to attain objectives. The supervisor is trained in the administrative skills necessary to achieve management's goals. If he does not possess the requisite skills, however, he can call upon management's technicians.

A natural leader can maintain his leadership, in certain groups, merely by satisfying members' need for group affilation. The supervisor must maintain his leadership by directing and organizing his group to achieve specific organizational goals set for him and his group by management. He must have a technical competence and a kind of coordinating ability which is not needed by many natural leaders.

A natural leader is responsible only to his group which grants him authority. The supervisor is responsible to management, which employs him, and, also, to the work group of which he is a member. The supervisor has the exceedingly difficult job of reconciling the demands of two groups frequently in conflict. He is often placed in the untenable position of trying to play two antagonisic roles. In the above instances, supervision is broader than leadership.

ORGANIZATIONAL INFLUENCES ON LEADERSHIP

The supervisor is both a product and a prisoner of the organization wherein we find him. The organization which creates the supervisor's position also obstructs, restricts, and channelizes the exercise of his duties. These influences extend beyond prescribed functional relationships to specific supervisory behavior. For example, even in a face-to-face situation involving one of his subordinates, the supervisor's actions are controlled to a great extent by his organization. His behavior must conform to the organization policy on human relations, rules which dictate personnel procedures, specific prohibitions governing conduct, the attitudes of his own superior, etc. He is not a free agent operating within the limits of his work group. His freedom of action is much more circumscribed than is generally admitted. The organizational influences which limit his leadership actions can be classified as structure, prescriptions, and proscriptions.

The organizational structure places each supervisor's position in context with other designated positions. It determines the relationships between his position and specific positions which impinge on his. The structure of the organization designates a certain position to which he looks for orders and information about his work. It gives a particular status to his position within a pattern of statuses from which he perceives that (1) certain positions are on a par, organizationally, with his, (2) other positions are subordinate, and (3) still others are superior. The organizational structure determines those positions to which he should look for advice and assistance, and those positions to which he should give advice and assistance.

For instance, the organizational structure has predetermined that the supervisor of a clerical processing unit shall report to a supervisory position in a higher echelon. He shall have certain relationships with the supervisors of the work units which transmit work to and receive work from his unit. He shall discuss changes and clarification of procedures with certain staff units, such as organization and methods, cost accounting, and personnel. He shall consult supervisors of units which provide or receive special work assignments.

The organizational structure, however, establishes patterns other than those of the relationships of positions. These are the patterns of responsibility, authority, and expectations.

The supervisor is responsible for certain activities or results; he is presumably invested with the authority to achieve these. His set of authority and responsibility is interwoven with other sets to the end that all goals and functions of the organization are parceled out in small, manageable lots. This, of course, establishes a series of expectations: a single supervisor can perform his particular set of duties only upon the assumption that preceding or contiguous sets of duties have been, or are being, carried out. At the same time, he is aware of the expectations of others that he will fulfill his functional role.

The structure of an organization establishes relationships between specified positions and specific expectations for these positions. The fact that these relationships and expectations are established is one thing; whether or not they are met is another.

PRESCRIPTIONS AND PROSCRIPTIONS

But let us return to the organizational influences which act to restrict the supervisor's exercise of leadership. These are the prescriptions and proscriptions generally in effect in all organizations, and those peculiar to a single organization. In brief these are the *thou shalt's* and the *thou shalt not's*.

Organizations not only prescribe certain duties for individual supervisory positions, they also prescribe specific methods and means of carrying out these duties and maintaining management-employee relations. These include rules, regulations, policy, and tradition. It does no good for the supervisor to say, *This seems to be the best way to handle such-and such*, if the organization has established a routine for dealing with problems. For good or bad, there are rules that state that firings shall be executed in such a manner, accompanied by a certain notification; that training shall be conducted, and in this manner. Proscriptions are merely negative prescriptions: you may not discriminate against any employee because of politics or race; you shall not suspend any employee without following certain procedures and obtaining certain approvals.

Most of these prohibitions and rules apply to the area of interpersonal relations, precisely the area which is now arousing most interest on the part of administrators and managers. We have become concerned about the contrast between formally prescribed relationships and interpersonal relationships, and this brings us to the often discussed informal organization.

FORMAL AND INFORMAL ORGANIZATIONS

As we well know, the functions and activities of any organization are broken down into individual units of work called positions. Administrators must establish a pattern which will link these positions to each other and relate them to a system of authority and responsibility. Man-to-man are spelled out as plainly as possible for all to understand. Managers, then, build an official structure which we call the formal organization.

In these same organizations employees react individually and in groups to institutionally determined roles. John, a worker, rides in the same car pool as Joe, a foreman. An unplanned communication develops. Harry, a machinist, knows more about high-speed machining than his foreman or anyone else in his shop. An unofficial tool boss comes into being. Mary, who fought with Jane is promoted over her. Jane now ignores Mary's directions. A planned relationship fails to develop. The employees have built a structure which we call the informal organization.

Formal organization is a system of management-prescribed relations between positions in an organization.

Informal organization is a network of unofficial relations between people in an organization.

These definitions might lead us to the absurd conclusion that positions carry out formal activities and that employees spend their time in unofficial activities. We must recognize that organizational activities are in all cases carried out by people. The formal structure provides a needed framework within which interpersonal relations occur. What we call informal organization is the complex of normal, natural relations among employees. These personal relationships may be negative or positive. That is, they may impede or aid the achievement of organizational. goals. For example, friendship between two supervisors greatly increases the probability of good cooperation and coordination between their sections. On the other hand, *buck passing* nullifies the formal structure by failure to meet a prescribed and expected responsibility.

It is improbable that an ideal organization exists where all activities are acarried out in strict conformity to a formally prescribed pattern of functional roles. Informal organization arises because of the incompleteness and ambiguities in the network of formally prescribed relationships, or in response to the needs or inadequacies of supervisors or managers who hold prescribed functional roles in an organization. Many of these relationships are not prescribed by the organizational pattern; many cannot be prescribed; many should not be prescribed.

Management faces the problem of keeping the informal organization in harmony with the mission of the agency. One way to do this is to make sure that all employees have a clear understanding of and are sympathetic with that mission. The issuance of organizational charts, procedural manuals, and functional descriptions of the work to be done by divisions and sections helps communicate management's plans and goals. Issuances alone, of course, cannot do the whole job. They should be accompanied by oral discussion and explanation. Management must ensure that there is mutual understanding and acceptance of charts and procedures. More important is that management acquaint itself with the attitudes, activities, and peculiar brands of logic which govern the informal organization. Only through this type of knowledge can they and supervisors keep informal goals consistent with the agency mission.

SUPERVISION, STATUS, AND FUNCTIONAL ROLE

A well-established supervisor is respected by the employees who work with him. They defer to his wishes. It is clear that a superior-subordinate relationship has been established. That is, status of the supervisor has been established in relation to other employees of the same work group. This same supervisor gains the respect of employees when he behaves in a certain manner. He will be expected generally, to follow the customs of the group in such matters as dress, recreation, and manner of speaking. The group has a set of expectations as to his behavior. His position is a functional role which carries with it a collection of rights and obligations.

The position of supervisor usually has a status distinct from the individual who occupies it: it is much like a position description which exists whether or not there is an incumbent. The status of a supervisory position is valued higher than that of an employee position both because of the functional role of leadership which is assigned to it and because of the status symbols of titles, rights, and privileges which go with it.

Social ranking, or status, is not simple because it involves both the position and the man. An individual may be ranked higher than others because of his education, social background, perceived leadership ability, or conformity to group customs and ideals. If such a man is ranked higher by the members of a work group than their supervisor, the supervisor's effectiveness may be seriously undermined.

If the organization does not build and reinforce a supervisor's status, his position can be undermined in a different way. This will happen when managers go around rather than through the supervisor or designate him as a straw boss, acting boss, or otherwise not a real boss.

Let us clarify this last point. A role, and corresponding status, establishes a set of expectations. Employees expect their supervisor to do certain things and to act in certain ways. They are prepared to respond to that expected behavior. When the supervisor's behavior does not conform to their expectations, they are surprised, confused, and ill-at-ease. It becomes necessary for them to resolve their confusion, if they can. They might do this by turning to one of their own members for leadership. If the confusion continues, or their attempted solutions are not satisfactory, they will probably become a poorly motivated, noncohesive group which cannot function very well.

COMMUNICATION AND THE SUPERVISOR

In a recent survey railroad workers reported that they rarely look to their supervisors for information about the company. This is startling, at least to us, because we ordinarily think of the supervisor as the link between management and worker. We expect the supervisor to be the prime source of information about the company. Actually, the railroad workers listed the supervisor next to last in the order of their sources of information. Most suprising of all, the supervisors, themselves, stated that rumor and unofficial contacts were their principal sources of information. Here we see one of the reasons why supervisors may not be as effective as management desires.

The supervisor is not only being bypassed by his work group, he is being ignored, and his position weakened, by the very organization which is holding him responsible for the activities of his workers. If he is management's representative to the employee, then management has an obligation to keep him informed of its activities. This is necessary if he is to carry out his functions efficiently and maintain his leadership in the work group. The supervisor is expected to be a source of information; when he is not, his status is not clear, and employees are dissatisfied because he has not lived up to expectations.

By providing information to the supervisor to pass along to employees, we can strengthen his position as leader of the group, and increase satisfaction and cohesion within the group. Because he has more information than the other members, receives information sooner, and passes it along at the proper times, members turn to him as a source and also provide him with information in the hope of receiving some in return. From this we can see an increase in group cohesiveness because:

o   Employees are bound closer to their supervisor because he is *in the know*

o   there is less need to go outside the group for answers

o   employees will more quickly turn to the supervisor for enlightenment.

The fact that he has the answers will also enhance the supervisor's standing in the eyes of his men. This increased status will serve to bolster his authority and control of the group and will probably result in improved morale and productivity.

The foregoing, of course, does not mean that all management information should be given out. There are obviously certain policy determinations and discussions which need not or cannot be transmitted to all supervisors. However, the supervisor must be kept as fully informed as possible so that he can answer questions when asked and can allay needless fears and anxieties. Further, the supervisor has the responsibility of encouraging employee questions and submissions of information. He must be able to present information to employees so that it is clearly understood and accepted. His attitude and manner should make it clear that he believes in what he is saying, that the information is necessary or desirable to the group, and that he is prepared to act on the basis of the information.

SUPERVISION AND JOB PERFORMANCE

The productivity of work groups is a product; employees' efforts are multiplied by the supervision they receive. Many investigators have analyzed this relationship and have discovered elements of supervision which differentiate high and low production groups. These researchers have identified certain types of supervisory practices which they classify as *employee-centered* and other types which they classify as *production centered*.

The difference between these two kinds of supervision lies not in specific practices but in the approach or orientation to supervision. The employee-centered supervisor directs most of his efforts toward increasing employee motivation. He is concerned more with realizing the potential energy of persons than with administrative and technological methods of increasing efficiency and productivity. He is the man who finds ways of causing employees to want to work harder with the same tools. These supervisors emphasize the personal relations between their employees and themselves.

Now, obviously, these pictures are overdrawn. No one supervisor has all the virtues of the ideal type of employee-centered supervisor. And, fortunately, no one supervisor has all the bad traits found in many production-centered supervisors. We should remember that the various practices that researchers have found which distinguish these two kinds of supervision represent the many practices and methods of supervisors of all gradations between these extremes. We should be careful, too, of the implications of the labels attached to the two types. For instance, being production-centered is not necessarily bad, since the principal responsibility of any supervisor is maintaining the production level that is expected of his work group. Being employee-centered may not necessarily be good, if the only result is a happy, chuckling crew of loafers. To return to the researchers's findings, employee-centered supervisors:

o Recommend promotions, transfers, pay increases

o Inform men about what is happening in the company

o Keep men posted on how well they are doing

o Hear complaints and grievances sympathetically

o Speak up for subordinates

Production-centered supervisors, on the other hand, don't do those things. They check on employees more frequently, give more detailed and frequent instructions, don't give reasons for changes, and are more punitive when mistakes are made. Employee-centered supervisors were reported to contribute to high morale and high production, whereas production-centered supervision was associated with lower morale and less production.

More recent findings, however, show that the relationship between supervision and productivity is not this simple. Investigators now report that high production is more frequently associated with supervisory practices which combine employee-centered behavior with concern for production. (This concern is not the same, however, as anxiety about production, which is the hallmark of our production-centered supervisor.) Let us examine these apparently contradictory findings and the premises from which they are derived.

SUPERVISION AND MORALE

Why do supervisory activities cause high or low production? As the name implies, the activities of the employee-centered supervisor tend to relate him more closely and satisfactorily to his workers. The production-centered supervisor's practices tend to separate him from his group and to foster antagonism. An analysis of this difference may answer our question.

Earlier, we pointed out that the supervisor is a type of leader and that leadership is intimately related to the group in which it occurs. We discover, now, that an employee-centered supervisor's primary activities are concerned with both his leadership and his group membership. Such a supervisor is a member of a group and occupies a leadership role in that group.

These facts are sometimes obscured when we speak of the supervisor as management's representative, or as the organizational link between management and the employee, or as the end of the chain of command. If we really want to understand what it is we expect of the supervisor, we must remember that he is the designated leader of a group of employees to whom he is bound by interaction and interdependence.

Most of his actions are aimed, consciously or unconsciously, at strengthening membership ties in the group. This includes both making members more conscious that he is a member of their group and causing members to identify themselves more closely with the group. These ends are accomplished by:

    making the group more attractive to the worker: they find satisfaction of their needs for recognition, friendship, enjoyable work, etc.;

    maintaining open communication: employees can express their views and obtain information about the organization.

giving assistance: members can seek advice on personal problems as well as their work; and

acting as a buffer between the group and management:
he speaks up for his men and explains the reasons
for management's decisions.

Such actions both strengthen group cohesiveness and solidarity
and affirm the supervisor's leadership position in the group.

DEFINING MORALE

This brings us back to a point mentioned earlier. We had said
that employee-centered supervisors contribute to high morale as
well as to high production. But how can we explain units which
have low morale and high productivity, or vice versa? Usually production and morale are considered separately, partly because they
are measured against different criteria and partly because, in some
instances, they seem to be independent of each other.

Some of this difficulty may stem from confusion over definitions of morale. Morale has been defined as, or measured by, ab-
sences from work, satisfaction with job or company, dissension among
members of work groups, productivity, apathy or lack of interest,
readiness to help others, and a general aura of happiness as rated
by observers. Some of these criteria of morale are not subject to
the influence of the supervisor, and some of them are not clearly
related to productivity. Definitions like these invite findings of
low morale coupled with high production.

Both productivity and morale can be influenced by environmental
factors not under the control of group members or supervisors. Such
things as plant layout, organizational structure and goals, light-
ing, ventilation, communications, and management planning may have
an adverse or desirable effect.

We might resolve the dilemma by defining morale on the basis of
our understanding of the supervisor as leader of a group; morale is
the degree of satisfaction of group members with their leadership.
In this light, the supervisor's employee-centered activities bear a
clear relation to morale. His efforts to increase employee identi-
fication with the group and to strengthen his leadership lead to
greater satisfaction with that leadership. By increasing group cohesiveness and by demonstrating that his influence and power can aid
the group, he is able to enhance his leadership status and afford
satisfaction to the group.

SUPERVISION, PRODUCTION, AND MORALE

There are factors within the organization itself which determine whether increased production is possible:

Are production goals expressed in terms understandable
to employees and are they realistic?

Do supervisors responsible for production respect the agency mission and production goals?

If employees do not know how to do the job well, does management provide a trainer--often the supervisor--who can teach efficient work methods?

There are other factors within the work group which determine whether increased production will be attained:

Is leadership present which can bring about the desired level of production?

Are production goals accepted by employees as reasonable and attainable?

If group effort is involved, are members able to coordinate their efforts?

Research findings confirm the view that an employee-centered supervisor can achieve higher morale than a production-centered supervisor. Managers may well ask what is the relationship between this and production?

Supervision is production-oriented to the extent that it focuses attention on achieving organizational goals, and plans and devises methods for attaining them; it is employee-centered to the extent that it focuses attention on employee attitudes toward those goals, and plans and works toward maintenance of employee satisfaction.

High productivity and low morale result when a supervisor plans and organizes work efficiently but cannot achieve high membership satisfaction. Low production and high morale result when a supervisor, though keeping members satisfied with his leadership, either has not gained acceptance of organizational goals or does not have the technical competence to achieve them.

The relationship between supervision, morale, and productivity is an interdependent one, with the supervisor playing an integrating role due to his ability to influence productivity and morale independently of each other.

A supervisor who can plan his work well has good technical knowledge, and who can install better production methods can raise production without necessarily increasing group satisfaction. On the other hand, a supervisor who can motivate his employees and keep them satisfied with his leadership can gain high production in spite of technical difficulties and environmental obstacles.

CLIMATE AND SUPERVISION

Climate, the intangible environment of an organization made up of attitudes, beliefs, and traditions, plays a large part in morale, productivity, and supervision. Usually when we speak of climate and its relationship to morale and productivity, we talk about the merits of *democratic* versus *authoritarian* climate. Employees seem to produce more and have higher morale in a democratic climate, whereas in an authoritarian climate, the reverse seems to be true or so the researchers tell us. We would do well to determine what these terms mean to supervision.

Perhaps most of our difficulty in understanding and applying these concepts comes from our emotional reactions to the words themselves. For example, authoritarian climate is usually painted as the very blackest kind of dictatorship. This not surprising, because we are usually expected to believe that it is invariably bad. Conversely, democratic climate is drawn to make the driven snow look impure by comparison.

Now these descriptions are most probably true when we talk about our political processes, or town meetings, or freedom of speech. However the same labels have been used by social scientists in other contexts and have also been applied to government and business organizations, without, it seems, any recognition that the meanings and their social values may have changed somewhat.

For example, these labels were used in experiments conducted in an informal class room setting using 11 year old boys as subjects. The descriptive labels applied to the climate of the setting as well as the type of leadership practiced. When these labels were transferred to a management setting it seems that many presumed that they principally meant the king of leadership rather than climate. We can see that there is a great difference between the experimental and management settings and that leadership practices for one might be inappropriate for the other.

It is doubtful that formal work organizations can be anything but authoritarian, in that goals are set by management and a hierarchy exists through which decisions and orders from the top are transmitted downward. Organizations are authoritarian by structure and need: direction and control are placed in the hands of a few in order to gain fast and efficient decision making. Now this does not mean to describe a dictatorship. It is merely the recognition of the fact that direction of organizational affairs comes from above. It should be noted that leadership in some natural groups is, in this sense, authoritarian.

Granting that formal organizations have this kind of authoritarian leadership, can there be a democratic climate? Certainly there can be, but we would want to define and delimit this term. A more realistic meaning of democratic climate in organizations is, the use of permissive and participatory methods in management-employee relations. That is, a mutual exchange of information and explanation with the granting of individual freedom within certain restricted and defined limits. However, it is not our purpose to debate the merits of authoritarianism versus democracy. We recognize that within the small work group there is a need for freedom from constraint and an increase in participation in order to achieve organizational goals within the framework of the organizational environment.

Another aspect of climate is best expressed by this familiar, and true saying: actions speak louder than words. Of particular concern to us is this effect of management climate on the behavior of supervisors, particularly in employee-centered activities.

There have been reports of disappointment with efforts to make supervisors more employee-centered. Managers state that, since research has shown ways of improving human relations, supervisors should begin to practice these methods. Usually a training course in human relations is established, and supervisors are given this training. Managers then sit back and wait for the expected improvements, only to find that there are none.

If we wish to produce changes in the supervisor's behavior, the climate must be made appropriate and rewarding to the changed behavior. This means that top-level attitudes and behavior cannot deny or contradict the change we are attempting to effect. Basic changes in organizational behavior cannot be made with any permanence, unless we provide an environment that is receptive to the changes and rewards those persons who do change.

IMPROVING SUPERVISION

Anyone who has read this far might expect to find *A Dozen Rules for Dealing With Employees* or *39 Steps to Supervisory Success*. We will not provide such a list.

Simple rules suffer from their simplicity. They ignore the complexities of human behavior. Reliance upon rules may cause supervisors to concentrate on superficial aspects of their relations with employees. It may preclude genuine understanding.

The supervisor who relies on a list of rules tends to think of people in mechanistic terms. In a certain situation, he uses *Rule No. 3*. Employees are not treated as thinking and feeling persons, but rather as figures in a formula: Rule 3 applied to employee X = Production.

Employees usually recognize mechanical manipulation and become dissatisfied and resentful. They lose faith in, and respect for, their supervisor, and this may be reflected in lower morale and productivity.

We do not mean that supervisors must become social science experts if they wish to improve. Reports of current research indicate that there are two major parts of their job which can be strengthened through self-improvement: (1) Work planning, including technical skills. (2) Motivation of employees.

The most effective supervisors combine excellence in the administrative and technical aspects of their work with friendly and considerate personal relations with their employees.

CRITICAL PERSONAL RELATIONS

Later in this chaper we shall talk about administrative aspects of supervision, but first let us comment on *friendly and considerate personal relations*. We have discussed this subject throughout the preceding chapters, but we want to review some of the critical supervisory influences on personal relations.

Closeness of Supervision

The closeness of supervision has an important effect on productivity and morale. Mann and Dent found that supervisors of low-producing units supervise very closely, while high-producing supervisors exercise only general supervision. It was found that the low-producing supervisors:

o check on employees more frequently

o give more detailed and frequent instructions

o limit employee's freedom to do job in own way.

Workers who felt less closely supervised reported that they were better satisfied with their jobs and the company. We should note that the manner or attitude of the supervisor has an important bearing on whether employees perceive supervision as being close or general.

These findings are another way of saying that supervision does not mean standing over the employee and telling him what to do and when and how to do it. The more effective supervisor tells his employees what is required, giving general instructions.

COMMUNICATION

Supervisors of high-production units consider communication as one of the most important aspects of their job. Effective communication is used by these supervisors to achieve better interpersonal relations and improved employee motivation. Low-production supervisors do not rate communication as highly important.

High-producing supervisors find that an important aid to more effective communication is listening. They are ready to listen to both personal problems or interests and questions about the work. This does not mean that they are *nosey* or meddle in their employees' personal lives, but rather that they show a willingness to listen, and do listen, if their employees wish to discuss problems.

These supervisors inform employees about forthcoming changes in work; they discuss agency policy with employees; and they make sure that each employee knows how well he is doing. What these supervisors do is use two-way communication effectively. Unless the supervisor freely imparts information, he will not receive information in return.

Attitudes and perception are frequently affected by communication or the lack of it. Research surveys reveal that many supervisors are not aware of their employees' attitudes, nor do they know what personal reactions their supervision arouses. Through frank discussions with employees, they have been surprised to discover employee beliefs about which they were ignorant. Discussion sometimes reveals that the supervisor and his employees have totally different impressions about the same event. The supervisor should be constantly on the alert for misconceptions about his words and deeds. He must remember that, although his actions are perfectly clear to himself, they may be, and frequently are, viewed differently by employees.

Failure to communicate information results in misconceptions and false assumptions. What you say and how you say it will strongly affect your employees' attitudes and perceptions. By giving them available information you can prevent misconceptions; by discussion, you may be able to change attitudes; by questioning, you can discover what the perceptions and assumptions really are. And it need hardly be added that actions should conform very closely to words.

If we were to attempt to reduce the above discussion on communication to rules, we would have a long list which would be based on one cardinal principle: Don't make assumptions!

o   Don't assume that your employees know; tell them.

o   Don't assume that you know how they feel; find out.

o   Don't assume that they understand; clarify.

20 SUPERVISORY HINTS

1. Avoid inconsistency.

2. Always give employees a chance to explain their actions before taking disciplinary action. Don't allow too much time for a "cooling off" period before disciplining an employee.

3. Be specific in your criticisms.

4. Delegate responsibility wisely.

5. Do not argue or lose your temper, and avoid being impatient.

6. Promote mutual respect and be fair, impartial and open-minded.

7. Keep in mind that asking for employees' advice and input can be helpful in decision making.

8. If you make promises, keep them.

9. Always keep the feelings, abilities, dignity and motives of your staff in mind.

10. Remain loyal to your employees' interests.

11. Never criticize employees in front of others, or treat employees like children.

12. Admit mistakes. Don't place blame on your employees, or make excuses.

13. Be reasonable in your expectations, give complete instructions, and establish well-planned goals.

14. Be knowledgeable about office details and procedures, but avoid becoming bogged down in details.

15. Avoid supervising too closely or too loosely. Employees should also view you as an approachable supervisor.

16. Remember that employees' personal problems may affect job performance, but become involved only when appropriate.

17. Work to develop workers, and to instill a feeling of cooperation while working toward mutual goals.

18. Do not overpraise or underpraise, be properly appreciative.

19. Never ask an employee to discipline someone for you.

20. A complaint, even if unjustified, should be taken seriously.

ANSWER SHEET

TEST NO. _____ PART _____ TITLE OF POSITION _____

PLACE OF EXAMINATION _____ DATE _____

(CITY OR TOWN)   (STATE)

RATING

USE THE SPECIAL PENCIL. MAKE GLOSSY BLACK MARKS.

	A B C D E		A B C D E		A B C D E		A B C D E		A B C D E
1		26		51		76		101	
2		27		52		77		102	
3		28		53		78		103	
4		29		54		79		104	
5		30		55		80		105	
6		31		56		81		106	
7		32		57		82		107	
8		33		58		83		108	
9		34		59		84		109	
10		35		60		85		110	

Make only ONE mark for each answer. Additional and stray marks may be
counted as mistakes. In making corrections, erase errors COMPLETELY.

	A B C D E		A B C D E		A B C D E		A B C D E		A B C D E
11		36		61		86		111	
12		37		62		87		112	
13		38		63		88		113	
14		39		64		89		114	
15		40		65		90		115	
16		41		66		91		116	
17		42		67		92		117	
18		43		68		93		118	
19		44		69		94		119	
20		45		70		95		120	
21		46		71		96		121	
22		47		72		97		122	
23		48		73		98		123	
24		49		74		99		124	
25		50		75		100		125	

ANSWER SHEET

USE THE SPECIAL PENCIL. MAKE GLOSSY BLACK MARKS.

	A B C D E		A B C D E		A B C D E		A B C D E		A B C D E
1	⁞⁞ ⁞⁞ ⁞⁞ ⁞⁞ ⁞⁞	26	⁞⁞ ⁞⁞ ⁞⁞ ⁞⁞ ⁞⁞	51	⁞⁞ ⁞⁞ ⁞⁞ ⁞⁞ ⁞⁞	76	⁞⁞ ⁞⁞ ⁞⁞ ⁞⁞ ⁞⁞	101	⁞⁞ ⁞⁞ ⁞⁞ ⁞⁞ ⁞⁞
2	⁞⁞ ⁞⁞ ⁞⁞ ⁞⁞ ⁞⁞	27	⁞⁞ ⁞⁞ ⁞⁞ ⁞⁞ ⁞⁞	52	⁞⁞ ⁞⁞ ⁞⁞ ⁞⁞ ⁞⁞	77	⁞⁞ ⁞⁞ ⁞⁞ ⁞⁞ ⁞⁞	102	⁞⁞ ⁞⁞ ⁞⁞ ⁞⁞ ⁞⁞
3	⁞⁞ ⁞⁞ ⁞⁞ ⁞⁞ ⁞⁞	28	⁞⁞ ⁞⁞ ⁞⁞ ⁞⁞ ⁞⁞	53	⁞⁞ ⁞⁞ ⁞⁞ ⁞⁞ ⁞⁞	78	⁞⁞ ⁞⁞ ⁞⁞ ⁞⁞ ⁞⁞	103	⁞⁞ ⁞⁞ ⁞⁞ ⁞⁞ ⁞⁞
4	⁞⁞ ⁞⁞ ⁞⁞ ⁞⁞ ⁞⁞	29	⁞⁞ ⁞⁞ ⁞⁞ ⁞⁞ ⁞⁞	54	⁞⁞ ⁞⁞ ⁞⁞ ⁞⁞ ⁞⁞	79	⁞⁞ ⁞⁞ ⁞⁞ ⁞⁞ ⁞⁞	104	⁞⁞ ⁞⁞ ⁞⁞ ⁞⁞ ⁞⁞
5	⁞⁞ ⁞⁞ ⁞⁞ ⁞⁞ ⁞⁞	30	⁞⁞ ⁞⁞ ⁞⁞ ⁞⁞ ⁞⁞	55	⁞⁞ ⁞⁞ ⁞⁞ ⁞⁞ ⁞⁞	80	⁞⁞ ⁞⁞ ⁞⁞ ⁞⁞ ⁞⁞	105	⁞⁞ ⁞⁞ ⁞⁞ ⁞⁞ ⁞⁞
6	⁞⁞ ⁞⁞ ⁞⁞ ⁞⁞ ⁞⁞	31	⁞⁞ ⁞⁞ ⁞⁞ ⁞⁞ ⁞⁞	56	⁞⁞ ⁞⁞ ⁞⁞ ⁞⁞ ⁞⁞	81	⁞⁞ ⁞⁞ ⁞⁞ ⁞⁞ ⁞⁞	106	⁞⁞ ⁞⁞ ⁞⁞ ⁞⁞ ⁞⁞
7	⁞⁞ ⁞⁞ ⁞⁞ ⁞⁞ ⁞⁞	32	⁞⁞ ⁞⁞ ⁞⁞ ⁞⁞ ⁞⁞	57	⁞⁞ ⁞⁞ ⁞⁞ ⁞⁞ ⁞⁞	82	⁞⁞ ⁞⁞ ⁞⁞ ⁞⁞ ⁞⁞	107	⁞⁞ ⁞⁞ ⁞⁞ ⁞⁞ ⁞⁞
8	⁞⁞ ⁞⁞ ⁞⁞ ⁞⁞ ⁞⁞	33	⁞⁞ ⁞⁞ ⁞⁞ ⁞⁞ ⁞⁞	58	⁞⁞ ⁞⁞ ⁞⁞ ⁞⁞ ⁞⁞	83	⁞⁞ ⁞⁞ ⁞⁞ ⁞⁞ ⁞⁞	108	⁞⁞ ⁞⁞ ⁞⁞ ⁞⁞ ⁞⁞
9	⁞⁞ ⁞⁞ ⁞⁞ ⁞⁞ ⁞⁞	34	⁞⁞ ⁞⁞ ⁞⁞ ⁞⁞ ⁞⁞	59	⁞⁞ ⁞⁞ ⁞⁞ ⁞⁞ ⁞⁞	84	⁞⁞ ⁞⁞ ⁞⁞ ⁞⁞ ⁞⁞	109	⁞⁞ ⁞⁞ ⁞⁞ ⁞⁞ ⁞⁞
10	⁞⁞ ⁞⁞ ⁞⁞ ⁞⁞ ⁞⁞	35	⁞⁞ ⁞⁞ ⁞⁞ ⁞⁞ ⁞⁞	60	⁞⁞ ⁞⁞ ⁞⁞ ⁞⁞ ⁞⁞	85	⁞⁞ ⁞⁞ ⁞⁞ ⁞⁞ ⁞⁞	110	⁞⁞ ⁞⁞ ⁞⁞ ⁞⁞ ⁞⁞

Make only ONE mark for each answer. Additional and stray marks may be counted as mistakes. In making corrections, erase errors COMPLETELY.

	A B C D E		A B C D E		A B C D E		A B C D E		A B C D E
11	⁞⁞ ⁞⁞ ⁞⁞ ⁞⁞ ⁞⁞	36	⁞⁞ ⁞⁞ ⁞⁞ ⁞⁞ ⁞⁞	61	⁞⁞ ⁞⁞ ⁞⁞ ⁞⁞ ⁞⁞	86	⁞⁞ ⁞⁞ ⁞⁞ ⁞⁞ ⁞⁞	111	⁞⁞ ⁞⁞ ⁞⁞ ⁞⁞ ⁞⁞
12	⁞⁞ ⁞⁞ ⁞⁞ ⁞⁞ ⁞⁞	37	⁞⁞ ⁞⁞ ⁞⁞ ⁞⁞ ⁞⁞	62	⁞⁞ ⁞⁞ ⁞⁞ ⁞⁞ ⁞⁞	87	⁞⁞ ⁞⁞ ⁞⁞ ⁞⁞ ⁞⁞	112	⁞⁞ ⁞⁞ ⁞⁞ ⁞⁞ ⁞⁞
13	⁞⁞ ⁞⁞ ⁞⁞ ⁞⁞ ⁞⁞	38	⁞⁞ ⁞⁞ ⁞⁞ ⁞⁞ ⁞⁞	63	⁞⁞ ⁞⁞ ⁞⁞ ⁞⁞ ⁞⁞	88	⁞⁞ ⁞⁞ ⁞⁞ ⁞⁞ ⁞⁞	113	⁞⁞ ⁞⁞ ⁞⁞ ⁞⁞ ⁞⁞
14	⁞⁞ ⁞⁞ ⁞⁞ ⁞⁞ ⁞⁞	39	⁞⁞ ⁞⁞ ⁞⁞ ⁞⁞ ⁞⁞	64	⁞⁞ ⁞⁞ ⁞⁞ ⁞⁞ ⁞⁞	89	⁞⁞ ⁞⁞ ⁞⁞ ⁞⁞ ⁞⁞	114	⁞⁞ ⁞⁞ ⁞⁞ ⁞⁞ ⁞⁞
15	⁞⁞ ⁞⁞ ⁞⁞ ⁞⁞ ⁞⁞	40	⁞⁞ ⁞⁞ ⁞⁞ ⁞⁞ ⁞⁞	65	⁞⁞ ⁞⁞ ⁞⁞ ⁞⁞ ⁞⁞	90	⁞⁞ ⁞⁞ ⁞⁞ ⁞⁞ ⁞⁞	115	⁞⁞ ⁞⁞ ⁞⁞ ⁞⁞ ⁞⁞
16	⁞⁞ ⁞⁞ ⁞⁞ ⁞⁞ ⁞⁞	41	⁞⁞ ⁞⁞ ⁞⁞ ⁞⁞ ⁞⁞	66	⁞⁞ ⁞⁞ ⁞⁞ ⁞⁞ ⁞⁞	91	⁞⁞ ⁞⁞ ⁞⁞ ⁞⁞ ⁞⁞	116	⁞⁞ ⁞⁞ ⁞⁞ ⁞⁞ ⁞⁞
17	⁞⁞ ⁞⁞ ⁞⁞ ⁞⁞ ⁞⁞	42	⁞⁞ ⁞⁞ ⁞⁞ ⁞⁞ ⁞⁞	67	⁞⁞ ⁞⁞ ⁞⁞ ⁞⁞ ⁞⁞	92	⁞⁞ ⁞⁞ ⁞⁞ ⁞⁞ ⁞⁞	117	⁞⁞ ⁞⁞ ⁞⁞ ⁞⁞ ⁞⁞
18	⁞⁞ ⁞⁞ ⁞⁞ ⁞⁞ ⁞⁞	43	⁞⁞ ⁞⁞ ⁞⁞ ⁞⁞ ⁞⁞	68	⁞⁞ ⁞⁞ ⁞⁞ ⁞⁞ ⁞⁞	93	⁞⁞ ⁞⁞ ⁞⁞ ⁞⁞ ⁞⁞	118	⁞⁞ ⁞⁞ ⁞⁞ ⁞⁞ ⁞⁞
19	⁞⁞ ⁞⁞ ⁞⁞ ⁞⁞ ⁞⁞	44	⁞⁞ ⁞⁞ ⁞⁞ ⁞⁞ ⁞⁞	69	⁞⁞ ⁞⁞ ⁞⁞ ⁞⁞ ⁞⁞	94	⁞⁞ ⁞⁞ ⁞⁞ ⁞⁞ ⁞⁞	119	⁞⁞ ⁞⁞ ⁞⁞ ⁞⁞ ⁞⁞
20	⁞⁞ ⁞⁞ ⁞⁞ ⁞⁞ ⁞⁞	45	⁞⁞ ⁞⁞ ⁞⁞ ⁞⁞ ⁞⁞	70	⁞⁞ ⁞⁞ ⁞⁞ ⁞⁞ ⁞⁞	95	⁞⁞ ⁞⁞ ⁞⁞ ⁞⁞ ⁞⁞	120	⁞⁞ ⁞⁞ ⁞⁞ ⁞⁞ ⁞⁞
21	⁞⁞ ⁞⁞ ⁞⁞ ⁞⁞ ⁞⁞	46	⁞⁞ ⁞⁞ ⁞⁞ ⁞⁞ ⁞⁞	71	⁞⁞ ⁞⁞ ⁞⁞ ⁞⁞ ⁞⁞	96	⁞⁞ ⁞⁞ ⁞⁞ ⁞⁞ ⁞⁞	121	⁞⁞ ⁞⁞ ⁞⁞ ⁞⁞ ⁞⁞
22	⁞⁞ ⁞⁞ ⁞⁞ ⁞⁞ ⁞⁞	47	⁞⁞ ⁞⁞ ⁞⁞ ⁞⁞ ⁞⁞	72	⁞⁞ ⁞⁞ ⁞⁞ ⁞⁞ ⁞⁞	97	⁞⁞ ⁞⁞ ⁞⁞ ⁞⁞ ⁞⁞	122	⁞⁞ ⁞⁞ ⁞⁞ ⁞⁞ ⁞⁞
23	⁞⁞ ⁞⁞ ⁞⁞ ⁞⁞ ⁞⁞	48	⁞⁞ ⁞⁞ ⁞⁞ ⁞⁞ ⁞⁞	73	⁞⁞ ⁞⁞ ⁞⁞ ⁞⁞ ⁞⁞	98	⁞⁞ ⁞⁞ ⁞⁞ ⁞⁞ ⁞⁞	123	⁞⁞ ⁞⁞ ⁞⁞ ⁞⁞ ⁞⁞
24	⁞⁞ ⁞⁞ ⁞⁞ ⁞⁞ ⁞⁞	49	⁞⁞ ⁞⁞ ⁞⁞ ⁞⁞ ⁞⁞	74	⁞⁞ ⁞⁞ ⁞⁞ ⁞⁞ ⁞⁞	99	⁞⁞ ⁞⁞ ⁞⁞ ⁞⁞ ⁞⁞	124	⁞⁞ ⁞⁞ ⁞⁞ ⁞⁞ ⁞⁞
25	⁞⁞ ⁞⁞ ⁞⁞ ⁞⁞ ⁞⁞	50	⁞⁞ ⁞⁞ ⁞⁞ ⁞⁞ ⁞⁞	75	⁞⁞ ⁞⁞ ⁞⁞ ⁞⁞ ⁞⁞	100	⁞⁞ ⁞⁞ ⁞⁞ ⁞⁞ ⁞⁞	125	⁞⁞ ⁞⁞ ⁞⁞ ⁞⁞ ⁞⁞